A Memoir of Growing up in
Southeast Alaska on the Eve of Statehood

RANEY "BUDD" WRIGHT

A FROG'S TALE
A Memoir of Growing up in Southeast Alaska on the Eve of Statehood

iUniverse books may be ordered through booksellers or by contacting:

iUniverse
1663 Liberty Drive
Bloomington, IN 47403
www.iuniverse.com
1-800-Authors (1-800-288-4677)

ISBN: 978-1-4917-9413-5 (sc)
ISBN: 978-1-4917-9414-2 (e)

Library of Congress Control Number: 2016905463

Print information available on the last page.

iUniverse rev. date: 06/17/2016

Table of Contents

A Frog Tale

The Woman Who Married a Frog

A Tlingit Tale as Retold by Mr. T

Near the mouth of L!ê'yâq Bay (Lah-ie-yak) sat a small Tlingit village, behind which was a lake. As with all such lakes it had many frogs. In the middle of the lake rose a swampy patch of ground on which many frogs would sit and sing.

Tlingit Village, Alaska State Library.

One day a daughter of the village chief picked up one of the frogs, as village girls were apt to do, and began talking to it saying,

"There are so many of you funny creatures I wonder if you do things like we humans do." She looked at its funny face and saw that the frog was looking deeply into her eyes. The girl quickly put the frog back in the pond and made her way back to the village thinking, *I wonder if men and women live among them like in the old stories.*

Sometime later she and her younger sister went into the forest looking for berries. Suddenly her younger sister lost sight of her for she had met a fine-looking man and they walked for a long time. Finally the man said, "May I marry you?"

Being the daughter of the village chief, she had rejected many fine suitors, but when she looked into his eyes she wanted to marry this man right away. Pointing toward the lake he said, "My father's lodge is just up there."

The girl replied, "How fine it looks."

When they approached the lodge the doors opened wide, but in reality the edge of the lake rose above the doorway, and they walked under the water. There the girl saw so many young people she did not think to go home again.

Meanwhile, when her younger sister got home she was asked by her mother, "Where is your sister?" She replied, "I thought she had already come home."

The villagers searched for her for a long time but could find no trace of her. Finally they gave up and her father had the drums beat for a death feast and the villagers cut their hair and blackened their faces in mourning.

The next spring the girl said to her children, "Go down to the village to see your grandmother and grandfather. Their lodge is in the middle of the village and you will know it when you see it. Tell them I have a message for them."

So her children went down from the lake to that house, but when they entered one of the chief's slaves called out, "Look at all those little frogs coming into our lodge!"

Then the children's grandmother said, "Throw them out." So the slave grabbed a broom and whisked them out the front door. When the children got back to their mother she asked, "Did you see your grandmother?" One answered, "I think it was her we saw. We went into the lodge you told us about and someone called out, 'Look at all those frogs! Throw them out.' and they did."

Then their mother said, "Tomorrow go back and see her again even if they throw you out. Tell her I have a message for her." So the next day the little frogs went back to the village and entered their grandmother's lodge once more. Again one of the slaves called out, "Those little frogs are here again! Shall I throw them out again?"

But this time the grandfather said, "Bring them to me. My daughter is missing and these little ones might be hers." He laid out a fox robe on the table and the grandparents placed the little frogs on it. The frogs crawled all over the robe and tried to talk to their grandfather, but only frog noises came out of their mouths. When the frogs had quieted down and were again seated in front of their grandfather, he gave them cranberries which they picked up with their forefeet and put into their mouths. When they did this their grandfather knew they were the children of his daughter.

Afterward, the villagers took all kinds of gifts to the lake to make the frog tribe feel good, hoping they would let the girl return to her parents. However, their efforts were in vain. Finally the chief said to his wife, "Make a martin-skin robe and place it beside the lake along with our daughter's other clothes." And that night she came to the edge of the lake with her high-cast husband in human form. She put on her robes and called out to her father. "Father," she said, "you and our people must come to live with us in this lake."

"Why?" asked her father. "Because the bear people are coming," she replied.

The next morning the chief called his clan together and told them what his daughter had said—that the bear people were coming and that his daughter wanted them to go live with the frog people in the lake.

"Who are the bear people?" asked the villagers, but the old man could not tell them because he too did not know who they were. The villagers were afraid to go into the black, cold waters of the lake so the old man gathered his wife, his other children, and his slaves and they went to the edge of the lake, which opened up for them, and they walked under the water.

The people of the village watched in wonder at this and some followed the old man into the lake, but many of the older people did not believe in such things and went back to their homes.

Months later a big war canoe with many sails and people who had shaggy hair, long beards and wore animal skins came into the bay. "These must be the bear people the woman spoke of" the villagers said.

By this time all the people who had followed their chief were asleep under the warm mud at the bottom of the lake and did not know what was happening to their village.

In the spring when they awoke the villagers, as small tadpoles, swam to shore and saw their village was no longer there. The bear people had taken all of the villagers away as slaves and burned down their homes, knocked over their totem and mortuary poles, and destroyed their great cedar canoes. The village people wept.

"Do not despair," the woman said. "You will go home again when the time is right."

Throughout the spring and into the summer, the people lived as tadpoles with the frog people. When their tails fell away and their legs grew they became fully grown frogs and again went to the edge of the lake. In the light of a full moon the villagers stepped out of the water and took back their human form. Together, they were able to rebuild their village. The people who believed in the woman who married the frog had been saved, and those who did not believe were taken away.

The woman stayed with the frog tribe at that place, L!ê'yâq, Bay so the frogs there could understand human beings when they talked to them. It was a Kîksa'dî (Kick-sa-di) woman who was taken by the frogs, so those people can understand the frogs when the moon is full. The Kîksa'dî have songs about the frog people, give frogs personal names, and use a frog as the emblem for their people. All the other people in the islands know about this.

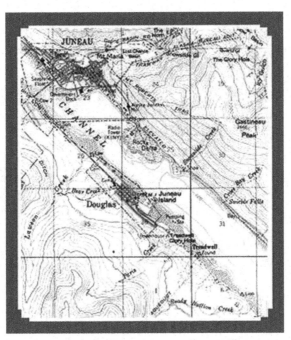

Map of Juneau -- Douglas

A Frog's Tale

The Wright Family.
My mother Florence "Kay", me,
youngest brother Richard,
middle brother John,
our dad SSGT William Wright

1956

Orders

In 1956, when I was ten, my father got transferred. Being an army brat, this wasn't anything new, but still the idea upset me a little. I mean geez, there I was at the top of my form—I was going to be on a Little League team, I was in Cub Scouts, and I had a bunch of friends. I even had a little paper route in the neighborhood where we lived. Maybe I was only in the fifth grade, but we moved around so much that Bryn Mawr Elementary was already my fourth school. All I wanted to do was stay where we were so I could be with my friends and have a real home. I wasn't crazy about moving again, and then my dad told us where we were going – Alaska.

Alaska! Wow that changed everything, for me at least. This would be a real move, Alaska. Just think there would be polar bears, eagles, seals, penguins, the northern lights, moose, whales, and glaciers (only kidding about the penguins.) The mountains alone were higher than any in the United States, oh yeah; did I mention that when I was ten Alaska wasn't even a state yet?

I don't think my mom was happy about the move. This would be our third move in six years, and besides she had a nice job and her friends too. It's hard to pick up and move all the time, and when you stop and think about it, Alaska was about as far away as you could get from anywhere, especially for a London war bride like me mum. The army even considered Alaska a foreign country and we had to get what seemed like a hundred shots before we could go "overseas."

My brother John and I dutifully packed our army foot lockers with all our worldly possessions while mom and dad made arrangements to sell our house. They also got our furniture packed and our car shipped out before we left for Seattle to stay with my aunt Nell and uncle Mick. In good army fashion dad flew to Alaska about two weeks before us to report for duty and find housing. In the meantime it's off we go; mom, me, my eight year-old brother John, and three year-old brother Richard to Fort Lawton, in Seattle, to get our shots—maybe not a hundred but a whole bunch.

On the last day of September 1956, we left Seattle for Juneau. My aunt and uncle took us to Seattle-Tacoma Airport, which was a lot different then. It was much smaller, but on the inside the lobby rose three stories high and had big windows which made the place seem bright and airy and not nearly as crowded. The airport had nice restaurants, shops, and an observation deck where people could go outside and watch planes take off and land. My uncle Mick suggested we—the kids—go up to the observation deck overlooking the runways and watch the planes.

The roar of those big propeller engines and the smell of their exhaust fumes, mixed with the heat coming off of the tarmac, heightened my senses, made me more excited, and made me breathe faster. My brother John, my cousin Mike, some friends, and I went outside to watch the action. For weeks John and I, excited about the trip, had studied up on airlines and airplanes. We were busy pointing out the planes on the tarmac and runways. "Looks like one of the new Electras," someone said. "Isn't that one of the new Western jets?" In response, we all yelled, "It's the only way to fly!" and raised our imaginary toasts of champagne.

There were all kinds of airplanes on the tarmac, and we had great fun pointing out both the airlines and the planes. Of course, we weren't the only ones doing that—other kids were running around shouting and pointing, and people were waving to passengers going to and from their flights.

But for us, the commotion stopped when Mike spotted a special plane, a Lockheed Super Constellation. "There it is," he said, pointing west toward the mountains. I think most of us thought it was about the prettiest plane ever built. I know I did—and still do. We forgot all of the other planes as we watched it circle around and come in from the south. Silhouetted, it looked like a flying banana—but with three tails.

"Whose is it?" somebody asked, not familiar with its markings.

We had to wait until it landed and taxied back to the terminal before John answered, "Pacific Northern."

"I know that one," I said as we watched it taxi to its gate and saw the ladder ramp roll out. "It's the other airline that flies to Juneau."

Of course there were other planes there: Douglas DC-5s and DC-6s, Convairs, Boeings, and Electras. We knew most of the airlines, too, such as Pan American World Airways, Pacific, West Coast, Continental, Eastern, Western, TWA (which we called Traveling with Angels) and many others that aren't around anymore.

"Look," John said, nudging me with his elbow. "I bet it's our plane coming in."

Pan Am Boeing 377 Stratocruiser.
Photo from Wikipedia

It was, and it was a beauty too—a Pan Am Boeing 377 Stratocruiser, the biggest passenger plane in the world. It had four huge engines, an upstairs, and a lounge downstairs—kind of like today's 747 but with a rounded nose. It was painted silver with blue and white stripes, and it had Pan Am's winged globe on its nose and stripes on its tail. It stood out from all of the other aircraft on the field, at least to me.

About that time my uncle came upstairs to get us. "Time to go," he said, and we scampered back down the stairs to the main lobby. About half an hour later we heard our flight announced: "Pan American World Airlines now boarding Flight 923 for Ketchikan, Juneau, and Fairbanks on Concourse Two."

We said our good-byes to my aunt and uncle, my cousin, and our friends who had come to wish us bon voyage. As we walked across the tarmac to our waiting plane my heart was pounding about as fast as I knew those giant propellers would be spinning in a minute or two.

Back then air travel was special, different, an adventure. Most people took the train when they traveled, but of course there were no trains to Alaska. Passengers dressed up to fly; the men wore suits and ties, and some wore fedora hats, which were in style back then. The women wore skirt suits or dresses with jackets. No one wore blue jeans or sweatshirts; air travel in the mid-fifties was elegant.

I don't know how high the plane flew—a lot lower than today's jets do. We could see the cities and towns below us: Seattle, Everett, and Bellingham in Washington, and Vancouver and Victoria as we continued north into Canada. After that it was mostly islands, forests, fjords, and an occasional fishing boat. We flew over the mountain wilderness of Vancouver Island then the countless islands along the British Columbian coast for hundreds of miles. The skies were sunshiny and clear all the way to our first stop at Metlakatla on Annette Island, an Indian reservation near Ketchikan.

By the time we neared Juneau it was getting dark, but from the air the terrain looked exciting and wild. Juneau is situated in a valley, with Gastineau Channel separating Juneau on the mainland from Douglas Island. Off to the east, behind the mountains, stretched the massive Juneau Ice Fields with hundreds of jagged mountain peaks thrusting up above a thousand square miles of ice. Alaska wasn't like any of my expectations, except maybe for the glaciers and mountains. I didn't think there would be any polar bears, penguins, or northern lights there (kidding about the penguins again), but there would be eagles, bears, and moose.

The Stratocruiser made a long slow descent between mountains on either side of us as it approached the airport north of the city. Juneau's airport was definitely nothing like Seattle's, just a one-story concrete block building with a waiting area and some storage sheds, not even a hangar. The Pan Am ground crew ran out the steps and we walked down to the parking apron. My dad waited behind the little fence in front of the so-called lounge.

After he gave my mom a big kiss, it was hugs all around, and then he said something like "Welcome to Alaska" with that big grin of his as we made our way into the waiting room to get our bags. The airport wasn't much to look at. Only four big planes landed per day: two Pan

Am flights and two Pacific Northern flights, one going north and one headed south for each airline. I guess they didn't need anything really fancy, but we were sure glad we made it after coming down between the mountains like we did. I immediately noticed one thing: the air sure smelled clean and crisp.

I spied our old black Ford waiting for us in the airport parking lot, that made me feel better. It and our furniture had arrived several days before. We all hopped in the car and drove south toward town, everyone talking at once, but when we got to Juneau's one and only stoplight (red-green, no yellow) dad turned right, and we went up and over the bridge I'd seen while flying in.

Although my dad worked in Juneau, housing there was in short supply, so we ended up in the little town of Douglas across the channel and south of Juneau. Dad was a telephone and teletype operator and worked in the Territorial Capitol Building with the Alaska Communications System (ACS). Back then all telephone calls to and from the territory were carried through underwater cables between Anchorage, Juneau, and Seattle. This was long before satellites and cell towers. My dad's job was to monitor the cable traffic and make sure all of the calls got through. The ACS also had responsibility for telephone and telegraph services out in the bush throughout the territory—, you know all types of communications.

Douglas, Alaska

It seemed a long drive to Douglas along the dark highway that first night. The trees came all the way down to the pavement, crowding the road and blocking any view of the water. When we got to Douglas all was quiet, even though it was early evening. There were two streetlights in town and we drove past them onto another dark, lonely stretch of road. We finally stopped in front of a single-story house built downslope from the road.

"Here it is," Dad said as he pulled onto a parking deck in front of the house. "I know it's not much to look at now but it'll look better in the morning."

House on St. Annes Street

We knew it was only temporary, until we could find something better in Juneau, but to be honest with you I don't think any of us were too thrilled about the place. It was on St. Annes Street, the main street south of town, but there were no other houses on our side of the street for blocks in either direction, and there were only two houses on the other side of the street. All the old houses had been torn down or burned down after the gold mines closed.

"Looks kinda lonely out here all by itself," I said as we walked to the front door.

"Looks pretty creepy, if you ask me," John said.

"Nobody asked you," Mom said, booting him with one of the suitcases. "Your father did the best he could and I'm sure this isn't the worst place we've lived."

Well she was wrong about that one. Upon reflection, I think that house on St. Annes Street was the worst place I've ever lived. It was old, cold, drafty, and it smelled funny. It had been added on to with two bedrooms on the south side; our parents got the front side and us kids got the one in the back. Our bedroom didn't get any heat because the only heat came from an old Sinclair oil heater in the living room and the heat didn't make it back that far. In the mornings my brothers and I would make a mad dash to see who could get to the heater first and be closest to its warmth when we got dressed. It was a good thing we had army arctic down comforters.

The one thing our creepy old house did have were great views. From our living room and kitchen we had a view to the northeast across the Gastineau Channel to the AJ Gold Mine south of Juneau. The mine worked its way up the side of the mountain maybe a thousand feet and ran about a mile along its face. Inside the mine shafts and tunnels ran for miles. The AJ Gold Mine was huge and unbelievably impressive with rust-colored corrugated siding that stood out from the gray rock, and at sunsets hundreds of glass windowpanes reflected a gold that the miners never dreamed of.

View north to AJ Gold Mine with parts of native village and Douglas waterfront in mid-ground.

The view to the south, from our bedroom window, was even better. We looked down the Gastineau Channel toward the ruins of the Treadwell Mine and beyond to Old Chief Taku Mountain on the mainland. Old Chief Taku, in native legend, is a sleeping Indian with his feathered headdress fanned out toward the channel, and he belonged to Douglas because he could only be seen from the South Douglas Highway. Our bedroom, did I mention it was unheated and had this big corner "L" shaped window; one single pane glass for each windows each – four-feet by four feet. When the icy winter Taku Winds blew up from the south, thick layers of ice formed on the inside of the glass! During those times, we really loved our army arctic comforters and when it really got cold, my brothers and I would retreat into the center of the house. Did I mention it had rats?

October may be like the worst time in the world for a kid to move. First of all, school has already started so you've missed any new-kid introductions or orientations and you mostly had to figure things out yourself. And who knows what you'll run into at your new school? One had to give up old friends and hope to make new ones quickly. Sometimes it's easy; sometimes it's a little harder. School's the first place to start making friends, then there's church, and Scouts.

Towns like Douglas—closed communities at the end of dead-end roads—had few families moving in or out in any given year, so all newcomers were a curiosity. That made it a lot easier to get to know people.

The Fifth Grade

That first day at school our parents took John and me to be registered. How embarrassing is that, walking into the office with your parents while all of the other kids looked at us. This new school didn't look all that great either. Back home my old school was really old—built in the 1890s—and had three stories. It was painted light green with white trim and looked like a real school. It had big tubes we got to slide down during fire drills. This new school looked old too but was made of gray concrete. To tell you the truth, it looked more like a jail than an elementary school.

Current view of Douglas School

Still, the first day of school can be exciting, hoping to spot a new friend or two and impress them with my urban sophistication. Of course it didn't happen that way. Miss Laurent, my new teacher, introduced me to the class and we had a break so I could meet my fellow students. The guys were nice, but after a quick "Hello," all the girls went over to see Rita's new hair style. This was a time when elementary girls had long hair and wore it in ringlets, pony tails, and pig tails. Well Rita had a new style called a DA and the girls were excited about it. Most of the boys, myself included, thought it looked stupid because it did. The back of Rita's head looked like a duck's ass. Well so much for my first day at school.

The next day John and I walked the six blocks to school by ourselves. At the bottom of St. Annes Street was another school building, the old Mayflower School, a native school not used anymore, and behind it the road to the Indian village. A couple of kids were walking toward us on their way to school and John asked me who they were. "A bunch of Indian kids, I guess," I said. He wanted to wait for them to catch up, but I wanted to get to school early, so the two of us walked on alone.

Douglas Elementary School ended up being pretty cool and it didn't take us long to make friends. The Indian kids we saw (they preferred being called Natives) lived on the street below our house on Sandy Beach Road.

I was in the fifth grade; John was in the fourth. I really liked my first classroom period and Miss Laurent, our fifth-grade teacher. She had us say the *Pledge of Allegiance* every morning, and on Mondays we got to sing a patriotic song. We had our choice: "The Star-Spangled Banner"; "America the Beautiful"; "My Country, 'Tis of Thee"; or my favorite, "Alaska's Flag." We each took turns choosing the song to sing, but you couldn't choose the same song as you did last time or the song we'd sung the week before.

Miss Laurent was primarily an English teacher, you know, grammar, spelling, poetry, and literature. She also liked baseball. I don't know how she did it, but like my first week there we were able to listen to the last two games of the '56 World Series between the New York Yankees and the Brooklyn Dodgers, the series with Don Larson's no-hitter! You see they didn't have live national radio in Juneau back then. Okay, I know Miss Laurent didn't do anything special to get those games, but just to be able to listen to the World Series in school was so cool. Of course the radio transmission was a special link through the ACS, and I like to think my dad had something to do with getting the live national feed for those games.

I had other teachers at Douglas, but one of the ones I remembered best were Mrs.

Olephent, the music teacher who gave up on me pretty early, as well she might, because I have absolutely no musical ear or talent. In the classes that didn't involve singing or the use of a musical instrument I did pretty good, but I was tone deaf and knew it.

Mr. Lewis, the art teacher, on the other hand let me explore my artistic side. Mr. Lewis's dad helped make the *Iwo Jima Marine Corps Memorial* in Washington, DC, and he in turn helped his dad with *The Prospector*, a statue at the Sitka Pioneer Home.

The teacher I remember most fondly was Mr. Green, our sixth-grade teacher and social-studies teacher. He allowed me to discover a love of history, geography, political science, and all that stuff.

One problem I had, had to do with the weather, as it always seemed to be cloudy and overcast, and in October the days were getting shorter. The high mountains on either side of the valley shortened the hours of daylight even more. I remember my first year at school, dark on the walk to school and dark when we came home again in the afternoon. After the second or third day John and I started waiting at the Mayflower School for the other kids and walked the rest of the way together.

Although we could see it from our bedroom window, a couple of weeks passed before John and I ventured to the street below us, Sandy Beach Road and the Native Village, yep, a real honest-to-goodness Indian village. Not the kind you see on TV or in the movies—there were no teepees, wickiups, or even longhouses; but all along the water side of the road on pilings sat a row of little houses and shacks (for lack of a better word). Most were unpainted, some had broken windows, and some were falling down. The village was where many of the Tlingit lived. In the olden days, before the Russians, the Tlingit were the mightiest of all the West Coast native tribes. They built great war canoes of cedar and raided as far north as Prince William Sound and as far south as the Queen Charlotte Islands. They had great villages with cedar longhouses and carved totem poles out front. But now, I thought it sad to see, they lived in unpainted shacks along the beach. Most of the houses were in worse shape than the one we lived in.

I don't think we, John and me, knew what prejudice was, but we could feel it in the way some kids treated others, and maybe that's the reasons most of the other white kids didn't go through the village to get to the beach and why they advised us to stay away too. However, we couldn't. First of all, being army brats, we weren't brought up to think that way and we had to go through the village to get to the beach—and there was hardly no way we were going to stay away from the beach. Secondly, native kids went to school too

John and I went trick or treating that first year but there were only two houses within walking distance of ours and they didn't expect kids so they didn't have anything. Of course mom stocked up on Halloween candy, but not a single knock on our door. All that candy for us, best Halloween ever. Thanksgiving got better because we had dinner with another army family in Juneau.

Me in my new Boy Scout uniform

For my 11th birthday my parents gave me a new Boy Scout uniform and a Remington .22

rifle, a real rifle. My dad would take me out to one of the highway quarries for target practice, to show me how to shoot and take care of the rifle. Being in the army he knew all about that stuff. Although a .22 isn't large enough to do much hunting it was an excellent rifle for small game like rabbits. Unfortunately there were no rabbits on Douglas Island, too much muskeg and swampy areas. Sometimes we went to the dump to shoot rats and when I got a little older my friends and I would go deer hunting. A .22 would take down the little deer common is Southeast Alaska.

Our first Christmas in Douglas was different because for the first time that I could remember we had no family or close friends to share it with. No big Christmas party at my aunt and uncle's house and fewer gifts under the tree. Back home you could just go downtown to Woolworth's, JJ Newberry's, or Penney's, something like that and buy a gift, but up here most things were ordered out of a catalog from Sears & Roebuck or Montgomery Wards and shipped up. Sometimes it took weeks to arrive so folks ordered gifts a month or two early. Also the families would go out into the forest and cut their own tree. We were used to getting ours from the neighborhood Chubby and Tubby Christmas tree lot. You know how good the trees look out in the woods, especially before you chop them down? Well the one we got looked great until we got it home and set up. That first Christmas tree left a lot to be desired, but at least we were all together as a family and when your dad's in the army that makes any holiday special.

Our first Alaskan Christmas tree

I considered myself a pretty good student, about average in most things and tried to stay out of trouble. It's not as if I went looking for trouble, or even that it followed me around, but sometimes I seemed to be in the wrong place at the wrong time (or as I liked to think of it as being at the right place at the best time).

"Hey you. You're the new kid right?'

"Ya, so what?" I replied carefully because I didn't know what they were up to.

"You wanta help us out for a minute or two?"

"Sure."

We were at the front door of the grade school, before the Christmas program, where small groups of people were mingling about watching the snow fall. They were high school students, maybe five or six, and I should have known better.

"All you have to do after the program is to make sure nobody goes around to the back of the school. Think you can do that?"

"We got a Christmas surprise for one of our buddies." added another kid.

Sounded good to me, why? I didn't know, and I didn't want to know. I did know that they were pulling some sort of prank, and as the new kid in school, I felt honored to be asked to be part of it and was more than happy to get involved. No one went to the rear of the school so after the program I walked home. Mom, Dad, John, and Richard had driven home earlier.

1957

We didn't find anything out until church on Sunday when we learned that somebody had stolen a teacher's brand-new 1957 Isetta, a little two-seater from Italy. My dad gave me one of those accusatory looks like he knew I had something to do with it. I shrugged my shoulder and gave him my best "I don't know anything" look. The Isetta was the only car like it in town, probably in the whole territory; it had three wheels and the whole front end opened up to get in or out. It was a pretty stupid thing to steal—a car everyone knew at a glance. I mean the thieves couldn't even drive it anywhere. This happened on a Friday night, the first week of Christmas vacation (yes, we had Christmas vacation and Easter vacation, and we had plays and skits and stories about Columbus Day, Halloween, Thanksgiving, St. Valentine's Day, St. Patrick's Day, and May Day).

The police looked all over town for that little car, but they never found it and I was as surprised as anyone else when on the first day of school they found the Isetta behind the stage curtains up on the gym stage. The high-school kids had picked the car up and carried it through the gym's back door and put it on the stage after the program. Okay, I lied; I went back and helped. I still think it was the best prank I have ever been part of.

One of the cool things at school was the use of Audio/visual (AV) equipment in classes. Our teachers would show us sixteen-millimeter filmstrips about subjects we were studying. I remember films about growing wheat in Kansas, dairy farming in Michigan, steel mills in Pittsburgh, and the opening of King Tut's tomb, that kind of stuff. We watched biographies of presidents, writers, and generals; clips from World War II and Korea; and films on railroads, airplanes, and transportation.

The filmstrip I remember the most was about bananas (probably because every time I eat a banana I'm reminded of it). It was titled something like *The Miracle of the Banana.* It showed plantation workers in Central America happily harvesting green bananas with their machetes. They loaded the big banana bunches onto donkeys which took them to little trains which in turn took the green bananas down the harbors where the happy longshoremen loaded them onto the United Fruit Company's steamships. They weren't singing the "Banana Boat Song," though—you know, "Come missa telleman, tally me banana. Daylight come, an' me wanna go home. Day, diddi day, diddi day, me say day, me say day-o."

The so-called miracle was supposed to be that the green bananas were placed on board different ships and sent to various ports like New Orleans, Baltimore, New York, San Francisco, and Seattle, where—through the miracle of modern agriculture, refrigeration, and transportation—the green bananas would arrive at the perfect state of ripeness for each city in the country. Wherever you lived, your bananas got to you at the perfect time. Of course Juneau wasn't part of the country, so our bananas were always like two weeks overripe by the time they got to us. Ever try to peel and slice a mushy brown banana for your cereal? Even in oatmeal with canned milk didn't even help.

A Different Lifestyle

The phones were strange—not the phones themselves (okay, the phones were a little strange too), but you called differently. Back home phone numbers had seven digits and had prefixes like PA for Parkway or RI for River or EA for Eastside, stuff like that. Juneau phones had four-digit numbers, but in Douglas we had only three-digit numbers and you had to call the operator. I think there were about five families on our party line. My dad, because of his job, was very strict about us listening in on other people's calls. It was part of phone etiquette.

On special occasions like my mom's or dad's birthday, New Year's, or some other big occasion, we got to go out for dinner. The best place we liked was Mike's Place in Douglas. It had like a saloon upstairs and a restaurant downstairs. We got to go downstairs. My dad always ordered a steak, mom usually got prawns, John and I usually got huge hamburgers, and three-year-old Richard got a little of everything. Me, I liked the fresh vegetables, but as my dad always reminded us, "Eat your meat; the vegetables are free."

We didn't get to go out much though, army pay for a Staff Sargent wasn't all that great back then and food was expensive. Everything had to be shipped up from Seattle by steamer. Most of the stuff we ate came out of a can: canned beans, canned vegetables (they even had canned corn on the cob), canned fruit, canned spaghetti, macaroni, ravioli. We also got canned meat like corned beef hash, ham, Dinty Moore beef stew, tuna fish, and Spam. Everything; even milk, which we mixed with powdered milk, came in cans. A lot of the cans had to be opened with a key that was inserted into a narrow strip of metal. The trick was to wind the key around the can without breaking the metal strip or the key coming loose. We also had fish caught locally or venison, mostly given to us by guys who were tired of salmon and venison.

My mom was a pretty good cook though. She'd lived in London during the war, when they rationed food, so she thought we had it pretty good in Alaska. About the only fresh vegetables we got though were what we called our "English vegetables" - you know potatoes, carrots, turnips, rutabagas, and parsnips.

Did I mention it rained a lot in Douglas? The rain had one good affect we did a lot of reading on rainy days. Nothing big you understand none of the classics—heck, I was only in the fifth grade. We did, however, have our literary outings when a new shipment of comic books arrived. Somehow word would get out and John and I would walk downtown with money in hand to join about half a dozen school kids at the drugstore. I think the object was to get as many kids as possible there at one time so we could each buy one comic book then sit around and share them. On nice days we would go outside and read them on the bench. Pretty soon a voice would ring out: "Trade a Mickey Mouse for a Superman." Then maybe someone would say, "I'm done with Sad Sack—who wants to trade?" I liked Batman and the Blackhawks. I still can't think of a better way to read and enjoy comic books than with a bunch of kids.

Sometimes, though, it rained so we would sit on the floor or the bottom shelf of the magazine rack and read. The room would slowly heat up from all the bodies and damp clothes. Pretty soon the windows would fog up and Mr. Poor or one of the clerks would come over and say, "Come on kids—give us a break." They would plead, but we would hold up our receipts to show we paid for the comic books we were reading. Just in case, someone would buy a candy bar or soda, or another comic to justify our not going out in the rain. Every time a new shipment of comic books arrived, we were there with our dimes in hand, and the clerks almost always welcomed us.

Winter turned into spring (see part on icy windows) and the school year trudged along. I had moved up from Cub Scouts to Tenderfoot in the Boy Scouts, mom was a Den Mother back in Skyway. We met in the Douglas School gym after school. I joined the Wolf Patrol, which was cool because we had a real wolf tail on our flagpole. There were other patrols like the Eagle Patrol, the Blackfish (Killer Whale) Patrol, the Bear Patrol, and the Raven Patrol. I also learned to play the snare drum for when we marched in and out of our meetings. Our Scoutmaster would have us line up by patrol and two Scouts would carry in the flags with me behind them, playing *rat-a-tat-tat, rat-a-tat-tat, tap-tap-tap* on the drum. (Mrs. Olephent hit the mark about my musical ability—or lack thereof.) Boy Scouts was great. I even got my own magazine in the mail, *Boy's Life*. I was the only one in our family who got a magazine. Scouts did things all year, even in the winter, which I found out in southeast Alaska meant more rain than snow. Still, there were some pretty big snowfalls when the road was closed and cut our little town off from the rest of the community. And of course there were the Taku Winds blowing up from the south.

"Students," Miss Laurent said, calling our attention away from whatever we were doing, "sometime this afternoon we will be having an earthquake drill." Looking around the room, she added, "Everyone knows what to do, right?"

They all nodded, having done this before. I did too, even though I'd never been in an earthquake drill. I figured it couldn't be much different that the air-raid drills we had back home; get on the floor under your desk and get as far away from the windows as you could. I figured an earthquake would be a lot safer than an air-raid because back home we lived between two of Boeing's largest airplane factories, Plant 2 in Seattle and the Renton Boeing Plant. Watching WWII movies you just knew that the bombers wouldn't stop dropping their bombs between factories just to miss our school. Yep, an earthquake seemed a much safer bet.

The Treadwell Mine

In school and at Scouts, we learned about mine safety—basically don't go near them. We learned about the mighty Treadwell Mine south of town—or what was left of it—and the AJ Mine on the mainland side of the channel south of Juneau. When operating between the 1890s and 1918 the Treadwell Mine on Douglas Island was the richest gold mine in the world, and the sole reason for Douglas to exist.

The mines were closed by the government during World War I. The government said they needed Doughboys in France more than they needed miners in far-off Alaska. After the war the Treadwell Mine never reopened. The same fate awaited the Sea Level Mine, the Excelsior Mine, and most of the other gold mines in Southeast Alaska. The AJ Mine lasted until the beginning of World War II, but then all the mines were closed, never to reopen.

Forty years later, by the time we moved to Douglas, the Treadwell Mine had fallen into ruin, as Alaska's weather is pretty harsh on man-made things. The big concrete buildings were there, but most of the tramways and smaller outbuildings were pretty much gone. *Danger* and *Keep Out* signs were posted all over the place, but of course those signs didn't stop us, nor the kids who went before us or those who came after.

The sandy beach and old buildings around the mine were just too great of a place to play. Outside, meaning the lower forty-eight states, we would have played cowboys and Indians, but that wasn't the game you played when you had real Indians playing, so we opted mostly for World War II, the allies against Germany. D-Day may have been our favorite 'cause we used the derelict boats on the beach and if the tide was out far enough the old pump house. The sounds of "Charge!" and "No fair—you're supposta be dead!" and "That-a-way, boys—take no prisoners!" rang across the sand and rocks.

The Treadwell Mine was the perfect place to play war games, or spend afternoons during the long summer days, exploring—carefully—around the mine site, old fishing boats, and other stuff on the beach. Then there was the "Glory Hole", a huge pit dug out by the miners to haul up the gold ore. The story is the Glory Hole got its name because so many miners went to their glory by being killed by rock falls and cave-ins. I can tell you one thing, it was one scary place. The water came up to about ten to fifteen feet from the top of the pit, which had sheer sides, and if anyone ever fell in they could never get out by themselves. For us, the challenge was to see who could get closest to the edge of the pit and drop a rock or something in. Of course the old building falling down all around us didn't add to our courage. Still, it was what us boys did.

We also went hiking, camping, and boating. Sometimes we just went out in the woods just to explore. I mean you couldn't get lost on the island—heck, all you had to do was walk downhill and sooner or later you'd reach either Gastineau Channel or Lynn Canal.

Later on we took to sailing around Douglas Basin, between the fishing docks and the Mayflower Island causeway, in old punts and little dinghies we painted to look like Viking ships and Indian canoes using window shades and old sheets as sails. If we really got carried away, and forgot the time, the tide would go out, and we would be stranded on the tide flats and have to drag our boats back to shore. Funny how heavy a little water-soaked dinghy gets when you had to drag it through wet sand.

The tides were really something, outside of the Bay of Fundy or New Zealand; I think Southeast Alaska has the highest tides in the world. At high tide you could step from the dock to the deck of some of the fishing boats, but at low tide you could only see the tops of their smoke stacks and trolling poles. In some places the tidal current was so strong that many fishing boats couldn't go against it. The tides in Gastineau Channel were not among the strongest in the region but it would have been easy for us in our little boats to have been carried away if we weren't careful. We always had to stay between the Douglas docks and Mayflower Island.

I don't know what my life would have been like outside—at eleven I don't think I gave it a thought. I do know us kids had it pretty easy. Our parents had lived through the Great Depression and two wars, World War II and Korea, so we were pretty much given a free rein. We were the first wave of the so-called baby-boomer generation, but of course we didn't know it at that time. We played on the beaches and in the woods, basically ran wild through town, or took our rifles hunting in the hills behind Douglas. We never got upset that we never shot anything, because hunting wasn't the real activity—being in the woods with our rifles and friends was. We played baseball in the summer and basketball in the winter. Mostly, our activities were loose and unorganized—whoever showed up played.

A Fishing Trip

That spring, 1957, my dad bought a boat, a real boat, from one of the army guys who got transferred, an old twelve or fourteen foot runabout with a big Evinrude outboard motor. On weekends when the weather was nice he would take John and me fishing in the channel in front of Douglas and our house. John once caught a halibut bigger than Richard, but he (Richard) didn't want to lie beside it so mom could take their picture. Mostly we'd trolled for salmon, but when we were done for the day and we would drop our lines to the bottom and try for halibut or snapper. Dad, of course, was good at fishing but I seemed to have problems with rat's nests, you know like when your line go out so fast it gets all bunched up in the reel? Happened to me a lot back then, still does. Dad and John would be happily fishing away and I would be mumbling under breath and wanting to cut the line. Of course you don't do that because you lose your leader, flasher, bait, hooks, and all.

We would only go out on sunny days because we had no canopy or cover of any kind if it rained, and of course it rained an awful lot. One thing we thought cool about the boat was that it had a beautiful old solid oak transom on to which we clamped the outboard motor. Everything worked fine as long as we trolled for salmon or just lay in wait for halibut.

That last day we took the boat out the weather was normal, cloudy and overcast. We were out past the Douglas docks, near Mayflower Island, and started jigging for snapper and drifting with the tide. Dad and John were aft talking among themselves while I sat in the bow trying to undo a rat's nest – as usual. The tide was running swift and before we knew it we were past the Treadwell Mine. Dad put his gear away and asked John to start the motor, poor John, as hard as he tried he could never start that outboard, and of course in the process flooded it.

Dad got a little upset and grabbed the starter cord and after a few sharp full pulls got the motor going and turned the boat towards home and revved up the throttle so we were soon headed towards the dock when, CRACK! That pretty oak transom split clear across the rear of the boat, just where the motor clamped on. Dad quickly throttled down to check the damage. The only thing holding the transom and the outboard to the rest of the boat were six or eight long brass screws. Dad was really upset and speaking some foreign language, French I think (I can't print what he was saying; he was in the army remember).

Things were getting serious now. If the boat slowed down water would come in from the cracks all around the transom and if we sped up the vibrations of the boat made the screws loosen even more.

"I don't think we're going to be able to make it back to the dock." Dad said grimly. "Boys, I think you had better put your life jackets on now. Bud, you help your brother."

I can tell you my heart sank. We were all quiet for a while as he maneuvered the boat towards shore near the mine's pump house. Finally he revved the motor as fast as it would go and plowed onto the beach. When the boat hit bottom it stopped. That's it, it stopped and we were thrown off balance and the transom and motor flipped up and over and tore the whole rear end of the boat off.

The three of us just sat there trying to catch our breath. Pretty soon some people who were on the beach at the time came running over to us to see if we were okay. We were, shaken but okay. A bunch of them helped us lug the boat up past the high tide line and carry the motor to the road. We got a ride home and mom was waiting for us at the door, news travels fast in a little town. The boat sat in our yard until we moved to Juneau then dad sold it to another solider.

Our poor boat after accident

Blood Brothers

John and I became good friends with of two of the native kids. They were among the kids we saw that first day we walked to school, Michael and Sonja. They lived in the house directly below us with their grandfather, Mr. T. Mr. T (his name was Russian and I never learned how to pronounce it let alone spell it) told us lots of old stories, like the fact his father served with the Russian American Company in Sitka when the U.S. bought Alaska from Russia in 1867. His father decided to stay in Alaska rather than go back to Czarist Russia. Czarist Russia—how cool was that?

Michael was John's age and they were in the same class at school and about a year older than Sonja. Their great-grandfather, the Russian, married a Tlingit woman and they moved to Juneau after the discovery of gold there in the 1880s. Mr. T grew up in the mining camps in Southeast Alaska. His daughter, Michael and Sonja's mother, married an Angoon man, but he got killed in the Korean War, so she moved back to her people in Sitka, while Michael and Sonja stayed with their grandfather in Douglas. But that was the way the natives did it; lots of times the kids were raised by aunts and uncles or grandparents instead of their own parents.

John and I liked to listen to Mr. T's stories and learn about Tlingits and the other Indians around Juneau. A larger native village was located in Juneau, just below Calhoun Street that included Eskimos, Aleuts, Haida, and Athabaskans. Many of the tribes had clans like Raven, Eagle, Blackfish, Wolf, and so on. I also learned why the natives didn't paint their houses—because the wood buildings had spirits and painting the wood planks would trap the spirits so they couldn't come and go as they were supposed to. Many of the older people still believed in the old ways—, like if somebody died in a house, they abandoned it and left it to the spirit of the person who'd died there.

I appreciated their customs and could understand the way they felt about their spirits and all, but still that kind of religion might have worked before the white men came, when clans and villages moved around a lot and they could build their villages just about anywhere they wanted. But now, with cities and everything, the shacks along Sandy Beach Road just didn't look good. Maybe that's why we were told to stay away from them.

Michael and I spent a lot of time together, mainly because he lived the closest to us. I had other friends, but mostly they lived on the north end of town. Nobody lived along the stretch of St. Annes where we lived. Somewhere along the line, somebody came up with an idea and said, "You know, you two should be blood brothers. You spend so much time together." I don't know who thought up this idea, but I know it wasn't mine! Of course John and Sonja were all for it, I mean; after all, it wasn't their blood. Sonja told her grandfather we were going to do it. I don't know if either of us took the idea seriously; I mean it sounded like a good idea at the time, but cutting ourselves with a knife? Not really big on that one. One afternoon Mr. T mentioned if we wanted, he would perform the ceremony for us. Having the ceremony performed by a real Indian chief made it seem like a cool idea again.

The Tlingit are a matriarchal society in that lineage is carried through the mother's bloodline, not the father's, which is why we thought of Sonja as a princess. Her royal bloodline came from her mother, grandmother, and her great-grandmother, all the way back to before the Russians came to Alaska. For the ceremony I had to have the names of my mother, Florence, my grandmother, granny Howl, and great-grandmother. Michael and I also had to exchange a gift unique to our culture. His tribe of course was Tlingit, and after much debate we decided since I was born in England mine would be English.

I think most eleven-year-olds would come home one day and ask, "Mum, can I have a puppy?" Not me, "Hey, Mum, can I become a blood brother with an Indian?" Besides we already had a dog, Droopy, who was more like John's dog than mine.

"That's 'Michael and I'."

"Right. Michael and I. Can we?"

"What?" she replied.

"Blood brothers, me and Michael. You know like in the movies."

"What does your father think of this?"

"I don't know. I thought I would ask you first."

After a moment or two, wiping her hands in a tea towel, she sat down and said, "Are you sure this is a good idea?"

"Oh sure," I said. "People do it all the time."

"I don't know. Maybe we should wait until your father comes home."

"But mom, it's a really cool idea. Michael and I would become blood brothers and I would be part Tlingit." I replied almost pleading because I knew my dad would say no unless I got my mom to agree."

The discussion at dinner that night between mum, dad, and me revolved around blood brothers and such. Dad knew about it, of course, but mom didn't know about such things, being English. John just sat at the table smirking like he knew I was going to get into trouble again. I was surprised that dad didn't reject the whole thing, although he didn't say I could do it, he didn't say I couldn't. I took that as a yes and over the next few days we planned the ceremony.

My mom was such a good sport about the whole thing. I think she kinda liked our involvement with the Indians, she still called them Indians. I mean, nothing like this would ever happen to any of my cousins back in England—or North Carolina, where my dad's side of the family lived, for that matter. She gave me a teacup and saucer set my aunt had brought over from England after the coronation of Queen Elizabeth II as my gift to Michael. It was a bone China cup trimmed in gold with the new queen's picture on the saucer and coronation coach on the cup. I'm sure my mom never thought we would do such a foolish thing and she wouldn't have to part with the cup and saucer set.

To tell you the truth, the ceremony was about what I had expected—just like in the movies. Mr. T told us not to worry 'cause he'd done it hundreds of times (I think he might have been exaggerating a little). Michael and I sat on the floor of his living room, our left arms resting on an ottoman facing each other. John and Sonja sat on the other two sides of the ottoman holding candles.

Mr. T started chanting in Tlingit and Russian as he walked around the room turning off the lights and closing the curtains. When the room was completely dark except for the two candles, he came to us and lifted our left hands so the palms were facing up, side – by – side. My heart pounded, just like when we were waiting to board the plane that seemed so many years ago. I closed my eyes, but Mr. T squeezed my hand to let me know I had to look. I peered through the darkness at Michael, his face lit only by the flickering yellow glow of the candles. I could tell he was nervous by the way he gritted his teeth and stared back at me. Mr. T removed the longest fish-fillet knife I'd ever seen from its sheath. Too late to back out now, I almost cried out for him to stop, but I swallowed hard instead. If Michael could do this, so could I. Mr. T held our palms tightly together and drew the blade across both hands in one simple stroke just below the thumb. Seeing the bright red blood ooze out of our skin was sorta hypnotic and it didn't hurt, that came later. He then folded our hands together and wrapped a white linen cloth around them.

"Make sure," he told us, "no blood comes through the cloth." We had to hold our hands together until the blood reached each other's heart. "Think," he said, "and remember what you have just done. You are now blood brothers forever."

We sat there, the four of us, Michael and I bound together, elbows resting on the ottoman, John and Sonja holding the candles for what seemed like ages. Finally, one of the candles went out (I think John blew his out), and Mr. T turned on the lights. As I blinked to adjust my eyes to the light, it seemed to me as if the living room had shrunk in size—a trick my brain played after gazing at the flames for so long and letting my mind wander so far. I think I really had been in a trance.

After removing the wrappings we looked to see how far the blood had soaked in—not far—and took that as a good sign. Sonja made us some Russian tea then we exchanged gifts. I gave him the coronation teacup set and he gave me a hand-carved totem of a frog.

"Welcomed to the Frog Clan," Mr. T said and welcomed me as a member of the Tlingit Nation, Auk (Sitka) Clan, and Frog Clan House. *Frog Clan! Whoa, a frog?* I thought they were of the clan of the Auk (little penguin-like birds) from Sitka or something like that. I don't know why I never thought they might be Raven, Eagle, or Bear, but being Frog never entered my mind either. Of course I didn't say anything—heck, I was still an Indian blood brother. Mr. T told us, John and me, that frogs were the most mystical of all clan totems; they were magical animals with special powers. Frogs were shape-shifters; they were travelers; and they could live on the land, under the water, and in trees.

"You know, Bud," he continued, "Every culture in every land has legends about frogs and their magical powers. Even white people have stories about frogs and princes and princesses. This, the most humble of all creatures, represents one of the most powerful of totems. "Let me tell you a story about the woman who married a frog." That was when Mr. T. and Michael told us the legend, but still, I thought, *A Frog?*

The blood brother thing happened during the summer so not many people saw the bandages on our hands, but word of it got out anyway. Most of the guys thought it was neat and even some of the girls asked to see the scar (a scab which healed much too quickly if you ask me).

I should note that I had a lot of other friends than Michael; he just lived closest to me. My friends Richard and Neil lived near the center of town, Jack lived in West Juneau, north of town, and Victor lived at the south end of town, down by the Treadwell Mine at the end of the road. Nobody lived in our part of town, along St. Annes Street. Of course Douglas only had four to five hundred residents living in it so we weren't too far apart.

Douglas didn't have much to offer in way of recreation; however it did have Little League. I think there were five or six teams between Juneau, Douglas, and Auke Bay. Douglas had two. I played on the Douglas Lions and played third base and left field. My batting was average for a sixth grader. We had wood bats and no helmets and played at the bottom of St. Annes Street, across from the Mayflower School. When we played teams on the Juneau side we went over as a team, and since most of our parents worked in Juneau we could stay after the game and ride home with them if we wanted.

Sometimes we would just walk or hitchhike back. Hitchhiking was easy 'cause usually the first car would pick you up. I mean who's not going to give a lift to a little kid wearing a baseball cap and carrying his bat and glove over his shoulder? Once in a while we would get a ride just to the Douglas side of the bridge and we would have to walk the rest of the way. The Douglas Highway had two lanes, no sidewalks, no street lights, and very little traffic.

The Sixth Grade

I led a pretty free and easy life that first summer, but now, going into the sixth grade, things began to change for no apparent reason. At the beginning of the school year elections for school offices were held and I got nominated for school treasurer along with this girl Michelle. I won the election but no biggie; I just had to learn how to keep books and stuff like that. Mom helped me with most of the work.

A different change faced us now. It occurred during the first week in October when the Soviet Union (not Russia, I missed that one on the test) launched *Sputnik*, the world's first satellite for the International Geophysical Year, and boy did it have the country in a tizzy. Actually the satellite was pretty cool; you could see it and *Sputnik II* when they flew overhead in the mornings or evenings when the low-angle sunlight would reflect off the sphere, and you could hear its radio signals on short-wave radios. *Sputnik* changed a lot of things. First, America wasn't in first place in something as big as space. The Soviets' education system must have been better than ours, and to prove it they had these shiny balls going around and around the earth. The news of *Sputnik* changed our teachers also. They began to push us harder with our studies. The changes really didn't affect me though; I studied the best I could but I would never be able to understand mathematics.

Another event occurred that month. October 18, 1957, marked the ninetieth anniversary of Alaska's purchase from Russia—a big deal in Alaska. The school put on a pageant for our parents and the town folk. Each grade put on a skit. Our class got to do a pageant on the history of Alaska. Each student had a role such as Russians, prospectors, fur trappers, lumbermen, fishermen, teachers, secretaries, and all the peoples who made up the territory. The natives in the pageant were real Alaskan

Natives. I got to be a prospector and when my turn came I jumped through the curtain onto the stage and said, "William Henry Seward bought Alaska from the Russians for $7,200,000 and already I've taken three times as much out in gold!" It was my first stage appearance.

I can honestly say that the sixth grade was my best ever year in school. I had a great teacher, Mr. Green, because of my travels became like the 'teacher's pet', which I liked because I got to be on the AV team and go around to the different classrooms and show the films. Life was going pretty well for me. I even had a girlfriend—sorta. Her name was Michelle, and she broke two bones in my foot one day at school, so I think she kinda liked me too. One day in class she got so mad at something having to do with Darwin, natural selection, and myopia that she slammed her books down on the floor and stomped out of the classroom. I sat behind her and had nothing to do with her little outburst, but being the son of a southern gentleman, I was picking up her books when she came back into the room and said, "I can do that myself—thank-you." She picked up her books and stomped out again—and this time she stomped her foot down right on top of mine.

But simple things can get complicated when you are in the sixth grade. It wasn't as if we were going out or anything—heck, outside of classes we hardly saw each other. I just kinda liked her and I think she kinda liked me. The funny thing about the election is that I don't remember ever doing any treasurer stuff except go to the student council meetings with the check book my mom helped me with. I don't even think the sixth-grade had any money.

I don't know how this thing between Michelle and me started, maybe with the Alaska-purchase skit at the beginning of the year. My mom had a real fox stole she offered for use in the pageant. Michelle got the role as a dance-hall gal (how appropriate I thought) and thought she should wear it instead of having the fur trapper showing it for the fur-trade industry. I thought the trapper should get it; after all, a trapper got it in the first place. So now she's upset with me for not taking her side, which leads to another lesson in adolescence – hormones (we'll come to that).

And if that weren't enough our, America's, first attempt at putting a satellite into orbit failed in spectacular fashion as the rocket ship exploded on take-off, never even leaving the ground. December 6th 1957, another day that will live in infamy.

Christmas and New Year's passed without any real events. We had gotten the knack of ordering out of catalogs with time to spare for the presents to arrive and our circle of friends had grown, and of course my dad was there to help us celebrate.

1958

The Purple Bow-Tie

I guess our feuding, Michelle and me, maybe got a little carried away, 'cause just before St. Valentine's Day Mr. Green made us stay after school to discuss any problems we may have had with each other. I'm sure he knew it as just juvenile infatuation, puppy-love; seemed more like puppy hate to me.

"Raney." he said, "I know your, and you too Michelle," turning to her sitting next to me, "can't keep on doing what you've been doing."

"I don't know what I've been doing." I answered. "It's her fault."

"It's not my fault you dingbat." Michelle answered, trying as usual to put the blame on me. "I didn't do anything wrong." she said turning to Mr. Green".

"'That's what I'm talking about. You're disruptive to the class."

"We're not the only ones." Michelle said.

"True as that may be, the two of you seem to cause me the most problems." He continued.

I'm sure he saw this type of behavior every year, and his solution for us was a dare. "I'll make you a deal." he said. "Michelle, do you know were Raney lives?" I thought it an odd question 'cause Douglas being so small everybody knew were everybody else lived.

"Sure." She replied, "In that creepy old house on St. Annes.

I started to say something, but saw the look in Mr. Green's eyes and bit my lip.

"Raney, do you know were Michelle lives?"

I almost said yes, but then I realized I didn't know, and had this feeling that I didn't want to know.

"I'm not sure. Up on Fifth or Sixth Street somewhere, I think." I said turning to look at her and sort of hunched my shoulders.

"Here's the deal and if you both agree I'll let this latest incident pass."

"But I didn't do anything wrong." I protested.

"Neither did I," Michelle chimed in. "Mrs. Neeley even said we didn't cheat after all."

The 'latest incident' involved Mrs. Neely, another of our teachers, who thought we had copied each other's answers during a health test. Michelle was, of course, an 'A' student, while I enjoyed my time spent in school studying things I wanted to learn, not necessarily what the teachers wanted us to learn. I never flunked any classes and I did not cheat! Anyway, we had this really hard exam on hygiene, etiquette, and stuff like that. Most of the class got four or five answers wrong, but Michelle and I only missed one each – the same question, 'How do you trim your toenails?' A = Cut them as an arc along the front of you toes. B = Cut then straight and even across the front of your nail. C and D I can't remember. We both missed the question and to this day I cut my toenails straight across the front which is the correct answer.

I thought Michelle was going to explode when Mrs. Neeley asked her if she copied my test because the proper assumption would have been that I had copied hers. Somehow a shouting match between the two of us got started which landed us in Mr. Green' classroom after school.

"Like I said, I'll make a deal with the both of you." he continued. "Michelle I want you to make Raney a necktie, and Raney I want you to go to Michelle's house and pick it up and wear it to school. Only for one day but it has to be all day. Do you agree?"

Neither knew what to say. My first thought that there should be some law against cruel and unusual punishment.

"Nobody needs to know why you are wearing the bow tie," he said to me, "and nobody needs to know that you knitted it." He said to Michelle. It will be between just the three of us."

"If you don't, I'll have to make note of it in your Permanent Record." he continued.

I really think he thought Michelle wouldn't knit me the tie and if she did I would never wear it to school, which somehow would put an end to our squabbling. No, I take that that back. I really don't know what he was thinking. Well, dang, if she did knit me a bowtie. I must confess it was difficult walking up to her house to get the tie and meeting her parents, but I did and wore it to school the next day and nobody noticed. Since then purple has not been my favorite color.

The Sixth Grade Continues

Hormones; a few weeks shortly after St. Valentine's Day we had a special A/V class, this one on sex education. Sex education! Heck, us kids didn't even say the word sex! One day the school's visiting nurse and Mr. Green told us we were going to see a couple of films, all the boys in one room, all the girls in another. Boy, I would never have thought Walt Disney would ever make an animated film on that subject!

Towards the end of the school year all the students in the school were told to line up by class and grade, with the older students first, then down to the first grade. We were to be part of the first nationwide assault on polio using Dr. Salk's new vaccine. Of course the nurses told us, "This won't hurt a bit," as they jabbed a needle into our arm. I think they had us older kids go first to show the younger ones the shots didn't hurt. Boy, were they were wrong on that one! There were more than one fifth and sixth grader (mostly girls) with tears in their eyes, but polio was a big thing back then and just about everybody knew someone on crutches or maybe somebody in an iron lung.

I learned to drive when I was in the sixth grade. On Sundays, after church, my dad would drive our old Ford out to the end of the North Douglas Road and let me drive. The gravel road ran about fourteen miles and dead-ended across from the airport. Few people lived out there and the road had little traffic to speak of. I could practice starting, stopping, shifting gears (hopefully without stalling), backing up, steering, and all that stuff. At least I was tall enough so my feet reached the pedals. Sometimes we'd also go out to the end of the road to have target practice in one of the gravel pits (pointing away from the airport).

As a family we liked to go on picnics. We'd pack up the old black Ford and take a drive. Sometimes we crossed over to the mainland and drive out to Auke Lake, but mostly we headed up North Douglas Road to my mom's favorite place and have our lunch, after which we would pan for gold. I never found out if what we were doing was legal since all the creeks around Juneau were supposed to be claimed.

I just hoped we wouldn't be arrested for claim jumping, but nobody ever said anything so I guess we were okay. Now days the tour companies have built gold panning stands, where we once panned, for the tourist. It's all part of their real Alaska adventure.

The creek waters were unbearably cold, especially when it came off the ice fields. Gold panning is easy, but hard work (does that make sense?). The easy part was finding a pool along the course of a creek where gold flakes could settle to the bottom because gold is heavier than sand and gravel. We had to gently shovel the gravel into our gold pan; that part was easy too. The hard part, squatting on your haunches or kneeling in the mud and gently swirling the pan in the cold water, washing out the sand and gravel made my back and legs hurt. My hands would be like ice, and my jeans would be sopping wet from splashing water on myself. We always found a little gold, which we'd pick out of the pans with tweezers, but at thirty-two dollars an ounce I could never imagine doing that for a living!

Eagle River Boy Scout Camp

During my second summer I got to go to the Eagle River Boy Scout Camp for two weeks. The Scout camp lay beyond the end of the highway north of Juneau, with an additional two-mile hike to the campsite. We had to make several trips to bring in all the camp gear in. We mostly slept in big canvas army tents, which were great until it rained (they were left over from the war and it seemed every one of them leaked). We had to get up at six o'clock in the morning (it was already daylight by then) to make our campfires, cook breakfast, and do all the other stuff one had to do in a camp. On chilly, foggy mornings nothing beats pancakes cooked on a hot griddle over an open fire or a big bowl of oatmeal for breakfast. Each troop took a day to do various camp functions. Patrols did different tasks, like splitting the wood for the stoves and fire pits, cooking meals for a hundred people, or washing the dishes. The camping experience was also a way to put into practice all the good stuff we had read about in our *Boy's Life* magazines.

Camp was neat 'cause there were troops from places like Sitka, Skagway, Wrangell, Petersburg, Ketchikan, and of course Juneau. At the end of our first week at camp one of the Scoutmasters came over to our campsite and said, "I need four volunteers—you, you, you, and you—to go with those other Scouts. You've just been enlisted into the Girl Scouts."

What? I thought. *Girl Scouts? No way!* But it was true. The Girl Scout camp was located on the far side of the river, sort of next to our camp, and the only way to cross the rushing glacier-fed torrent of a river was to take a little ferry back up at the end of the road. Like our camp, all the gear had to be packed in, and because Boy Scouts are such gentlemen, it fell upon us to do the legwork. The girls' parents parked at the end of the road and we hauled their gear onto the little ferry and pulled it across the river.

We did this five or six times until we got all the stuff on the north bank, then we helped the girls pack it down to their camp. It wasn't that bad and they fed us lunch. When we got back to our camp some of the other guys were ribbing us about joining the Girl Scouts. My only comment was "I tried to get in but flunked the physical."

Thus began the name games; Rene, or Ranee, stuff like that. The girls seemed not to mind Raney, but the guys began massacring it.

The second week we had a campout in which each patrol would go out and set up a campsite in a designated area. It had to be a protected campsite with a latrine, and a safe cooking area. Our patrol, Wolf, picked an area near (under) some huge cedar trees. One of the Scoutmasters came by and evaluated our site. "Think this place will work?" he asked.

"Sure," we said, confident of our scouting skills.

"If your camp is under the trees, how can you cook your dinner," he asked, "without burning down the trees?" He then moved on to inspect the next campsite.

We thought it over and moved our campsite, this time to a hillock not far from the cedar trees.

When the Scoutmaster passed through again, he stopped and looked at the trees where our old campsite had been and then back at our new campsite. He asked, "What will you do when the winds come up tonight and you're all exposed up here?"

So we moved again and settled for a large sandy area in the lee of the hillock and pitched our tents once more. Let's be honest here, we already had dug our privy and we weren't in the mood to dig another, besides it was getting late. When the Scoutmaster came around for the third time he looked at our campsite but didn't say a thing and went on checking the campsites of the other patrols.

About two or three o'clock in the middle of the night my feet got wet—then my sleeping bag, then everything else. We had pitched our tents on the sandy tidelands, and when the tide came in we were flushed out! The Scoutmaster and a few other counselors were there waiting for us as we scrambled out of the water. His only comment was "All you had to say was, 'We'll cook our meals in the open away from the trees.'" Then he and some of the other scouts we had woken with all the noise we made helped pull us and our gear up onto dry land.

Tide flats at Scout Camp

One of our favorite games was Capture the Flag, and given the long summer days, these games often lasted well into the evening. The sun set around eleven thirty, and the twilight lasted until after midnight, but the game continued until one side won. Once I captured the Gold team's flag and made a mad dash for the Blue team's headquarters. Instead of running along the dune crests I opted to charge across the sandy flats yelling, "I've got it, I've got it!" which caused about two dozen gold scouts to come after me. Seemed the tide had come in and as I splashed into the icy water I lost the flag, but by then a lot of us were splashing about that night. Black sand, black water and incoming tides did me in again.

Camp wasn't all games of course. We learned scouting lore, knot tying, Morse code, how to do our laundry in metal buckets, and of course, wilderness survival and first aid. Outside, in the lower forty-eight states, an easy way to find north if you were lost in the woods was to look for moss on tree trunks or rocks 'cause moss grew on the north side in the shade. In Southeast Alaska, because of the overcast skies and massive amounts of rain, moss grew everywhere, all around the tree trunks and all over most rocks. In the lower forty-eight to look for Polaris you scanned the horizon until you spotted the Big Dipper then looked for the end of the cup and up to the North Star. In Alaska you just kinda threw your head back and rolled your eyes because the North Star was right there above you.

One of the most important wilderness survival tips to know if you ever got lost, other than walking downstream to salt water, was magnetic deviation. Magnetic deviation, as every Boy Scout knows, is that the magnetic north pole is not at the North Pole but someplace in northern Quebec or Baffin Island, someplace like that. If you are on the east coast it isn't much of a problem as those locations are north of you, but as you move farther west and farther north this knowledge becomes really important. Juneau, being so far west and north and having so much iron ore around, has a north magnetic-compass reading of east by northeast!

Among other things, wilderness survival also meant eating strange things off the beach, but we learned an old native saying: "When the tide is out, the table is set." We found clams, mussels, crabs, seaweed, and more. We also had smoke wood—, but maybe I shouldn't mention it. Smoke wood are short, sun-dried, sticks of driftwood with holes bored in them by sea worms— that we tried to smoke like cigars. The counselors could never tell if we'd been smokin' because we always smelled like wood smoke anyway.

Scout camp, in a way, put an end to the free-spirit days we'd had before. We learned first aid and the art of triage, which was a sobering aspect of our training, as we realized that sometimes some will live, some will die, and you might have to make the choice. We learned the old way of camping, but the future lay in the stars with more emphasis on science and math. Boy Scout Camp showed us we were responsible for our actions, our planet and emphasized the importance of working together and learning our way in the world.

Moving to Juneau

I got some good news when I got back from scout camp: "Pack your stuff. We're moving." My dad said. "We found a place for us to live, in Juneau itself." We were all glad to be moving out of our old house in Douglas, but our new house, which was about eighty years old, was a lot smaller. At least it wasn't exposed to the frigid Taku Winds, and the best part, I had a room to myself. It was not a real room just a storage closet barely big enough for an army bunk. I had to open the door to put my feet on the floor, but it was all mine and I could hang my model planes from the ceiling and have my ship models on the shelves without my brothers breaking them.

*View from our house looking
west showing Mt. Jumbo*

Our new place was at the top of Third Street, next to the Bergman Hotel. The street was gravel then and so steep cars couldn't drive up it, just down, and it had boardwalk steps on either side. But boy did we have a great view of the city and the mountains on Douglas Island. We lived just a few blocks from downtown and I could walk to my new school, the library, the movies, and the Teen Club

I also discovered radio at this time. Of course I listened to radio all my life, but radio is such an easy thing to take for granted. In Juneau we had two radio stations and I learned to appreciate radio as something special. In the evenings, KINY would play rock 'n' roll music and old radio dramas, such as *Inner Sanctum, Fibber Magee and Mollie, Red Rider,* and *The Shadow,* shows like that. On weekends they broadcast the news in English, Russian, and then Tlingit, and the late-night weather reports were at least an hour long, reporting winds, tides, temperatures, and weather conditions all the way from Yakutat south to Ketchikan for the fishermen, loggers, and others making a living in the wilderness. I usually fell asleep about the time they got to Five Fingers Light.

*View from our house looking
north with Bergman Hotel
showing the face of the Knoll*

TV was another matter; we didn't get it in Douglas because there was no cable service and it came on at three in the afternoon and went off the air around nine at night. All the shows were two weeks late because the film canisters were flown from Seattle to Ketchikan, then to Juneau. I don't know if they went any farther north, but I can imagine them arriving in Nome months later. We had only two channels, but what the heck—at least we had TV.

One of the downsides of our move was we had to change churches, switching from the Methodist Church in Douglas to Holy Trinity

Dredge Lake as it had shallower and warmer water. I could drive around the parking areas and kinda show off.

Boating on Dredge Lake,
our swimming hole

I think I liked our skating outings in winter best. I tried joining the older kids playing hockey on Auke Lake whenever I could, but I really didn't know the game, and the best I could hope for was to chase the puck across the frozen lake when a shot went out of bounds. Other times John and I would put Richard on a sled and tow him over the ice. If we were far enough away from our parents we would play crack the whip and send Richard's sled gliding across the ice as it spun in circles. After a really – really, cold spell, when the ice had frozen over the creeks and streams, us kids liked to skate up and down them among the ice- and snow-covered tree branches. On skating parties we roasted hot dogs and got Polar Bears to drink to keep us warm. A Polar Bear is hot cocoa spiked with peppermint schnapps.

John skating on Auke Lake

Did I mention it rained in Juneau too? Fortunately our house was just a few blocks from the library. On rainy days I read, on cold overcast days I read, I read when it snowed, and occasionally, I read even when the sun shined. I read every book in the Hardy Boys,

Tom Swift Jr., and Nancy Drew series. I read some Edgar Rice Burroughs, Jules Verne, and H. G. Wells and *The World Book Encyclopedia* almost cover to cover (why is the "P" volume the thickest?), except the long articles about states and countries, mostly the short articles about wars and biographies. Comic books were still high on my reading list, too, but unlike in Douglas, the folks at Percy's Drugs Store were not going to allow us to sit around their store reading and sharing comics.

Sometimes when the weather was bad, my brothers and I would sit at the kitchen table and play board games like Parcheesi, Pirates & Travelers, or checkers. Or we would sit on the floor in front of the oil heater and play cards using one of footlockers as a table. By the time he was six, my little brother Richard had become a pretty wicked Pinochle and poker player.

The Fourth of July Parade was, of course, the biggest event of the year. Most of the logging and fishing camps closed, and those folks came to town. When we lived in Douglas we drove over to Juneau for the parade and other holiday events, but now we were there. One thing our family did every year was put flowers on the veterans' graves for Memorial Day and I got to sell VFW Buddy Poppies. Halloween was a big deal for us teenagers even though we were too old to go trick-or-treating by this time, but still I had to take my little brothers around—you know how that works. Our small house didn't allow for much entertaining, so we usually shared Thanksgiving and Christmas dinners with other army families in town.

Juneau was the territorial capital and the big city, third largest in the territory, with about six thousand people, whereas little ole Douglas claimed about four hundred. In Douglas we could walk most everywhere, as the town probably covered less than a square mile. Not so in Juneau, it stretched for several miles along the eastern shore of Gastineau Channel and onto on the flat lands made up of mine tailings, then up the sides of the mountains. The streets were narrow and curvy with lots of steep hills that often dead ended to flights of stairs leading to homes higher up. The great thing about Juneau is that most of the gold rush buildings were still standing because Juneau never had the Big Fire. The old wood frame office buildings and apartments were still standing, as were a number of elegant homes as well as a lot of older not so elegant houses.

The pace of life was slow. The only ways to get to Juneau was by either plane or boat as there were no road connections to the outside world. Sure we had the capital but not much of the government happened here, as most governmental functions were handled at the federal level out of Washington, DC, or maybe Seattle, or Portland. Gold Creek which runs through town is a prime example. The first gold strikes were found along its banks, Gold Creek – duh. The creek flooded all the time and after one too many floods the city fathers (or maybe the federal government) decided to pave the creek. They channeled it in a concrete flume, six feet deep by four feet wide, from where it flowed out of the Evergreen Bowl, a high valley behind town, all the way down to salt water. I think that took all of the fun out of a creek run through the middle of town—they should have made it maybe four feet deep and twelve feet wide. At least it would have looked better.

The big city park was located in the Evergreen Bowl and had tennis courts, picnic tables, and all the other amenities city parks have like slides, swings, that kinda stuff. The best thing about the park was that it had an outdoor pool built by the WPA. It had its problems besides leaking, at the beginning of the week, when the water was clean it was generally too cold to swim in, and by the end of the week when the water warmed up it was too dirty, you know with little kids and everything. To get to the park we walked on an old mine trestles leading up to the bowl between two mountains. The park was close to where we lived and we could walk to it so we spent a lot of time there.

The large knoll between the Evergreen Bowl and Juneau is where we used to mountain climb—it wasn't really mountain climbing but the next best thing in our minds. The front had a sheer face that rose (or fell, depending on where you were standing) maybe six or seven hundred feet. While I never made it up the face, I made it to the top plenty of times—sometimes without falling into the salmonberry bushes and Queen Anne's lace (which I found out I was allergic to) after tumbling down the mountainside for forty or fifty feet on my third or fourth clime. In places, the climbs were really quite challenging, but we were teenagers and quite up to the challenge.

Unlike Douglas, we had two movies in Juneau, the Capitol and the Coliseum. The Coliseum on Front Street was where we went most of the time 'cause it had Saturday matinees with serial movies from the 1940s, a cartoon, and the main picture, all of which cost less than two-bits. Sometimes they would have promotions when it cost like seven 7Up bottle caps, or maybe a dozen egg cartons to get in, stuff like that. The Capitol was the other theater and for some reason it seemed to get the better pictures, like in 1959 when the movie industry decided to have a world premiere in each state. The Capitol Theater got the premier of *John Paul Jones*. I got to go the second night, almost as good as the real thing.

More changes were on the way. Junior high is a time when teenagers are hit by more challenges than there are points on the compass. Changes come from all directions; changes in education like moving from classroom to classroom amid a bunch of kids you didn't know and trying to make new friends and not lose the ones you have. The school administration didn't help either, with its prep school challenge, and let us not forget those screaming hormones. My name, Raney, was still getting a bad rap at school and after trying to substitute something else; Ray, Walter, my middle name, and Walt, somebody even suggest Sonny, but in the end I fell back on my family's nickname, Bud. Of course this had its own challenges as some teachers and adults called me Raney, others Bud. Most of my friends used Bud.

Finding Home

It was a time when you realized that while Mickey Mantle is the greatest baseball player alive, you would never see him play (even if you didn't live in Alaska) and no matter how good you are the chances of you making the "team" were pretty slim. Maybe baseball wasn't the most important thing after all. A big change came to me one summer afternoon when some of my buddies came up to the house and asked if I wanted to get into a pickup ball game down on Willoby Street. That might have been the first time that being a frog affected my life. I was about halfway through *Wind in the Willows* and had to decide whether I wanted to play ball or finish the book. I chose the book. I now realize that I could have gone to the game and finished the book later, but at the time it seemed like a make or break decision.

Wind in the Willows is more than an adventure story about animals; it is a story about home and friends. I suspect most boys who read the book think of themselves as Mr. Toad (in England he is a toad, but if he were in Alaska he would be a frog) who was the most adventuresome of the lot. All of the characters had their homes, which they cared deeply about: Toad Hall and the dens and burrows of Rat, Mole, and Badger.

I, on the other hand, never had a home. I lived in houses, but a house does not make a home—not a home with deep family roots and memories of childhood. The concept of a home as a place where one longed to be when one is away was foreign to me. My home was where my family was; the spiritual rather than physical feeling of a house versus a home eluded me. I think that is why I chose the book over the ball, to explore this concept deeper. It didn't hurt that the characters reminded me of my friends, and that on some level I felt we were all living the great adventure. I have often thought about how my life might have been different if I had just picked up my mitt and joined the game but I was beginning to think of Juneau as my home.

My Last Fight

This happened shortly before my big fight. I suspect that I got into as many fights as any boy my age, whatever that age might have been. Fighting seemed natural for army brats, as we had to prove ourselves to the other kids on every move. Like the time after we got transferred to Fort Brag, North Caroline, I had to defend my honor against two other kids on the block. Okay, so I ended up headfirst in a Dixie Dumpster, but in the end we became best of friends. Mostly, I didn't start fights but got sucked into them by coming to the aid of my brother or a friend. It seemed most of the time the fights occurred in connection with some sporting event, particularly baseball or basketball, when our blood was hot to begin with. Sometimes I won, sometimes I lost, but nobody ever kept score as far as I knew. My last fight in Juneau I won, but lost so much more in many other ways.

We were playing pickup basketball in the courtyard between the junior-high building and Fifth Street Elementary. The basketball court was asphalt, plus we tended to play a bit rough to begin with. Several of us, myself included, kept getting knocked to the ground by these two older kids on the other team. That wasn't all that unusual until one of them outright shoved one of our team players to the ground. That was the end of the basketball game as we all started pushing each other around, started swinging our fists, and calling each other names. One of the other players started making fun of my name, calling me *Rayneeee*. I hated that. He was a big black kid, and in the heat of the fight I called him a nigger. I knew that if he wanted to he could have pounded me into the ground any time he wanted.

All of a sudden the fighting stopped, and everyone stared at me. I knew the word *nigger* was offensive, as were *spick, wetback, kraut,* and a lot of the other ethnic names kids called each other. But I had no idea of the power—the hate—that that word invoked. Luther—that was his name, simply walked off the court and went home. No other words were spoken. I had won the fight, but in doing so I had broken a silent code and I knew it. Within a minute or two the schoolyard was empty.

When my dad got home from work I told him about the fight and what I had said. Being from the South I thought maybe he would be easy on me. He wasn't. He told my mom to hold dinner and we walked over to where Luther lived. Dad stood on the sidewalk outside their picket fence as I walked up to the front door and knocked. This happened more than fifty years ago, and I still find it hard to write about. Luther's dad opened the door and looked at me with such a disapproving look. There were only two or three colored families in the community and they hoped to have gotten away from stuff like that.

"I've come to apologize, sir." I said as I stood at their front door.

He let me in, and in front of his entire family I said, "I sorry Luther." and turning to the rest of the family, I add, "My father did not bring me up to be prejudice. I don't know what I can say, not only the using the word but also the thought behind it."

Looking at Luther, I continued, "You know me, that was not the real me. Please accept my apology." He just nodded. Then I left with my head hanging low and I walked home with my dad.

To this day I feel that making that apology was one of the toughest things I have ever done. If this were a story, a novel, we would have made up and become the best of friends, but that never happened. The look on his face when I called him that name has never left me. Words are more powerful than any of us can imagine. I lost interest in most sports after that incident, although I still played baseball now and then.

We re In

On July 4, 1958, the Alaska Statehood Act was signed by President Eisenhower allowing for Alaskan statehood. Did I say that kinda casually? I was walking along Calhoun Street on my way to the library, and all the cars passing were honking their horns. Finally, one of the passengers yelled at me, "We're in!" I have to tell you for a junior high kid that was like the biggest thing ever, especially if you consider the last time a territory became a state was way back in 1912. To be in a territory when it became a state! WOW! The new US flag would have forty-nine stars. I still have my 49 star flag I got back then stowed in my footlocker.

About a week after the big news about statehood we were sitting at home watching TV, a local game show called *Ringo*. Really, it was Bingo, but they couldn't call it that – you know, copyright stuff. The deal was that when you went to the grocery store and bought groceries, you got a Ringo playing card; so many cards for each ten dollars' worth of groceries, and each card had a different serial number printed in the free space. The Ringo callers on TV would turn a wire basket, pull out a ball and read the number. If you got a Ringo, you would call the station and give them the number from the free space. If the numbers matched you won a prize, such as a bag of groceries or a big turkey or ham, stuff like that. I mean it wasn't a big production, and the sets were low budget. The Ringo callers sat on folding chairs behind two card tables with the bingo cage next to them.

We were watching and playing along, like we did every week when the whole house started to shake — **EARTHQUAKE!** It was not the first since we'd moved to Alaska, but it was the biggest so far, and everything started shaking— not only in our house but in the TV studio too.

Things were shaking so hard the Ringo basket fell off the table and the backdrop behind the callers fell down. A stagehand ran onstage and handed one of the callers a note which probably said, "Earthquake." The announcers told us, "**It's an Earthquake,**" as if we couldn't tell. "**Keep calm; don't panic.**" as they tripped over themselves knocking over the tables and chairs trying to get out of the studio. It was the first time I had actually seen people in a real panic, scary but hard not to watch.

Earthquake Rule #1: Stay inside in case power lines are knocked down. I can't remember Earthquake Rule #2 'cause we were all running outside. Our house, being so old, we were not sure it would survive such a big quake. Silly us—our old house had probably survived a hundred such quakes. Being at the top of 3rd Street, we could look down over Juneau and the scene outside was like a dream. Even though the quake struck in the evening we had enough light to see the telephone poles swaying in unison, like some crazy dance, and at the far end of the street (on the bluff where the new State Office Building is) stood the old three-story wood-frame Territorial Prison building, swaying in the opposite direction as the telephone poles, and way off in the background, Mount Jumbo, on Douglas Island, gave the illusion that the trees were swaying in unison with the telephone poles. It was a surreal vision to be sure.

We stood there for two or three minutes eye glued to the scene in front of us, back and forth swayed the telephone poles. We actually expected the lines to snap in front of us, but they didn't. They did in other parts of the community though, as power went off all over town, ours included, another evening by candle light. So much for my earthquake drills.

The earthquake lasted for more than two minutes, and it was the biggest one I'd ever been in—a 7.2 on the Richter scale. We learned the next day where the quake had occurred: Lituya Bay, just north of Glacier Bay. Lituya Bay is shaped like a capital *T*, with the bottom going into the Gulf of Alaska. The earthquake caused hundreds of thousands of tons of rock and ice to crash into the water at the top of the *T*, and the sloshing water created a tidal wave that crested over 1,720 feet high, higher than the Empire State Building, the tallest building in the world, and the highest tidal wave ever recorded. For weeks afterward there were pictures and stories about the earthquake in the newspaper. It was quite the event.

My Role in Pictures

Big things were in the works with statehood looming and the Lituya Bay Earthquake was soon old news. During the summer, parts of *Ice Palace* were filmed in Juneau. It was billed as a big spectacular movie starring Richard Burton and Robert Ryan. One day, they were filming on the steps of the Capitol Building, where our dad worked, and as John and I were coming out of the building after getting our mail, the director Vincent Sherman, asked, "Would you two kids like to be in the movies?"

Duh. "Sure." we said, I mean who wouldn't want to be in a movie with Richard Burton? Actually, I don't think we knew who Richard Burton was, but we weren't going to turn down the chance to meet a real movie star. The director asked us to go back inside and walk down the Capitol steps on cue. He filmed the scene a few times at different angles— we would walk down the steps as Mr. Burton either walked or ran up the steps. The crowd across the street got bigger with each take. Finally they were done, and the crew packed up. That was it—not even an opportunity for an autograph, a word of thanks, or anything. I don't remember seeing our scene when I finally saw the movie; it seemed we had been edited out. A grand start at a movie career ended abruptly.

The Seventh Grade

In the fall of '58 the Douglas seventh-grade class moved to the "new" Juneau Junior High because a new high school opened down by the boat basin and we inherited their old building. Maybe I should note we were the last class to graduate from Douglas Elementary School because construction on the new Gastineau School was finished. Anyway, we all matriculated, as the saying goes, and we became Crimson Cubs at Juneau Junior High School, on Fifth Street. Although I went to classes with my Douglas friends, I soon lost touch with most of them outside of school activities since they had to take the bus to and from school.

In addition to our class from Douglas, seventh graders from the Juneau and Auke Bay elementary schools also moved to J.J. High. Those of us elected to our old schools' Student Councils still held their officers and a new school administrator asked the incoming seventh-grade Student Council to write a new school song and design school crest. I think his name was Mr. Adams from Springfield, Massachusetts (or his name could have been Mr. Springfield from Adams, Massachusetts—I never got his name straight). He had come to us from a fancy New England prep school (whatever that was) and he wanted his "new school" to have a fancy song and crest too.

He had this song in mind: "Give me some men who are stouthearted men, / who will fight for the right they adore." Something like that from some old opera he liked. He wanted new words to reflect Alaska and all that stuff. Our song committee (which did not include me, as I knew nothing about music) had a song made up for the tune that kind of worked. I—along with other artsy types—had better luck with the new crest, which we based on the face of a bear cub. The high school was known as the Crimson Bears and junior high was known as the Crimson Cubs. The new crest looked like the army's Alaska Command, except it had the face of a bear cub and didn't have the star.

Mr. Whatever-His-Name-Was totally rejected our new song and kept the old words. The rejection especially hurt those who were on the song committee since they felt we were far from being stout-hearted men and had worked so hard on the new lyrics. He didn't even like the new crest. It wasn't really a crest but more of a badge, but still pretty good for seventh graders.

This new guy got off to a bad start, in our eyes at least. We sorta got our revenge though (even though we didn't do a thing). As the story goes, Mr. Adams-Springfield went back to New England during the Thanksgiving or Christmas holiday taking with him some of the school's property, such as typewriters, a movie projector, a mimeograph machine, and other office equipment. At least we didn't have to deal with him anymore. That's my story, and I'm sticking to it. After that incident, being on the Student Council kind of lost its luster, so I didn't run for a seventh-grade position. Just like that, a brilliant career in politics nipped in the bud.

Continental Drift

I had it pretty easy in the seventh grade, except the damn Soviets launched another *Sputnik*, and the administrators gave another big push to science and mathematics. But for me, it was another project from the 1957 International Geophysical Year that caught my interest: Continental Drift. Who ever heard of such a crazy idea—the continents floating on the oceans like ice flows? Well, a Danish weatherman who observed the ice flows around Greenland in the early 1900s— that's who. By the 1970s, the hypothesis had become pretty much accepted, but in 1957 it was still considered a wild theory and I still remember the famous quote in support of the theory: "as any junior high school boy knows, Africa and South America were once joined." Well, as a junior-high boy, I could see they had once fitted together, not perfectly, but pretty closely. Our social-studies and geography teacher was a radical and believed in continental drift long before it became accepted. For one of our class assignments we had to cut up world maps and try to put the continents back in their original positions. We had lots of heated debates in the classroom and at home (while doing homework) about that one. For extra credit several of 'advanced' geography students tried to fit Italy back to Africa. It's funny; evolution was pretty much accepted in school. I guess we didn't have any fundamentalist churches in town to challenge Darwin.

1959

Alaska Statehood Stamp

Alaska officially became the forty-ninth state on January 29, 1959, and what a fireworks display we had that night down at the Coast Guard sub port. Supposedly, the city fathers used up all of the fireworks bought for the next Fourth of July. I don't know if that rumor was true or not, but what a show on a cold January night!

However, our world came crashing down less than a month after the euphoria of statehood. By our world I mean us teenagers who were into Rock 'n Roll music. Buddy Holly, the Big Bopper, and Frankie Valens were all killed in an airplane crash. Juneau was an isolated community and for is kids Rock 'n Roll music was one way that we could connect with teenagers outside. We all listened to the music at the same time, not delayed like television. Elvis Presley, Fats Domino, Jimmy Dean, and others were our connection to the outside and Buddy

Holly was number one in my book, and most of my friends too. We were devastated. There are no musical groups around today that have the sway over teenage music like Buddy Holly and the Crickets.

Memorial Day

Every spring some of kids, Army and Coast Guard brats mostly, would sell VFW Buddy Poppies on Memorial Day, May 31st (the American Legion sold poppies on Armistice Day, November 11th, because it marked the end of WWI, when the Legion was founded). Now that we were on the Juneau side of the channel John and I decided we'd join some of the other kids who were out selling poppies for their dads. Actually we weren't selling them but rather taking donations for the VFW.

Each kid who had done this before had their best place to sell their poppies, like standing in front of the grocery store and asking shoppers as they entered if they would like a poppy; Thebadou's Market being a favorite spot. John decided to go to Erwin's since mom worked there and she would buy a poppy even if nobody else would. Us kids got our supply of paper poppies at the VFW Post behind the

Baranof Hotel and scattered, each to their special place. Since I had no idea where to go I headed to the corner of Franklin and Front Streets which was the main intersection in town and would be the best place to ask people if they wanted a Poppy. When I got there I ran into Jack who was just at a lost as what to do as I was.

There we were when a guy comes out of the Triangle Club dugs in his pocket, gave me a nickel or maybe a dime, and told us if we really wanted to make some money we should go inside and ask the vets sitting at the bar. Well, of course, we weren't old enough to go into the Triangle Club, and I had never been in a bar without my dad. Jack and I looked at each other and said, "What the heck?" We had nothing to lose.

With our Poppy cans in one hand and a bunch of bright red Poppies in the other, we bravely pushed open the door and went inside. The bar was dark, smoky, and smelled of stale beer and urine. Not really the kind of place I would like to spend a spring afternoon, or any afternoon for that matter. The bartender looked up at us from behind the bar but didn't say anything.

"Anybody want to buy a Buddy Poppy?" I asked in my most-mature voice. Not one person answered—no one even turned around to look at us. Well, like we said, we had nothing to lose.

"Outta here, you kids!" the bartender barked. "We don't allow no beggin' in here."

I had no idea what to expect, but that wasn't it. As we started to back out the door, almost in unison, all the guys at the bar turned saying, "I'll take one." In less than ten minutes we collected more money than we had gotten standing for an hour outside on the street corner. One of the guys even suggested we try some of the other bars down the street. The one thing Juneau had was bars.

As the saying goes, "Nothing ventured, nothing gained." So for the rest of the day Jack and I hit all the bars on South Franklin Street, including the Pioneer Bar, the Alaska Bar, and the Red Dog Saloon, as far as Erwin's Case Lot Grocery, where my mom worked. She gave us a bite to eat, and then we headed back up the street to the lounge of the Baranov Hotel. Almost everyone in the bars bought a poppy. That afternoon we collected about $50.00 in pennies, nickels, dimes, and quarters. Some guys even put a dollar bill or two in the cans.

Even as a kid, I always considered that event one of the highlights of my years in Juneau. I was thirteen years old and I'd hit most of the bars in downtown Juneau. I also learned something about people—not right away but more as a reflection, so to speak. I don't recall any women in the bars, and the patrons seemed to fall into two groups: the older workers (the miners, fishermen, and loggers who had the day off) and the younger veterans. Of course, back then, almost every male over the age of twenty-five had served in either WWII or Korea. It just seemed a little sad for these guys to be spending such a nice day in a bar, and while we were not supposed to be there, our presence seemed to cheer them up a little.

South Franklin Street across from Erwin's Case Lot Market, where mom worked: Photo from Army Corps of Engineers

And yes, we did get into trouble for this one. Even though Jack and I collected the most poppies donations, neither the VFW nor the Juneau Police were thrilled with a couple of juveniles spending all Memorial Day bar hopping along South Franklin Street.

The Excitement of Statehood

Statehood brought special and exciting things. *The Ed Sullivan Show* taped a special from Juneau; was the first time a network, CBS, had done a major TV program from Alaska (except maybe for the Bob Hope USO Christmas Shows). CBS planned to shoot the show from the Red Dog Saloon, which was a real saloon back then, located on the west side of South Franklin Street, but the original saloon was too small for all the cameras and lights, so CBS moved the Red Dog Saloon across the street into a larger space (only real Juneauites knew the difference. I knew because Jack and I went into the real Red Dog Saloon when we were selling Buddy Poppies).

My parents were able to get tickets for the night of the show, and dad got my mom a beautiful new gown, hat, and gloves. When they aired the show several weeks later we watched as our parents sat at a table with their friends on *The Ed Sullivan Show*.

Other things were still happening all around us that didn't involve statehood. Actually, after the first glow of statehood wore off, it was pretty much back to life as usual. School went on and on until it was finally summer again. There were picnics and outings with new red-white-blue and Alaskan flag designed paper plates and stuff.

First Rising of 49 Star Flag on July 4th 1959: Photo from Alaska State Archives

July 4th! Excitement was in the air as our country's new forty-nine-star flag was raised in front of the library. Governor Stepovich was there, along with the army, Coast Guard, VFW, and American Legion. Bands played, and the Liberty Bell in front of the Capitol Building was rung forty-nine times, once for each state. The fireworks were even better than those in January.

The parade was the largest Fourth of July parade ever held in Juneau. It started on

South Franklin and went up to Front Street, down Gold Street, and out to Thebadou's Market. All kinds of people lined the streets. The loggers and miners from the camps all came to celebrate, as did most of the fishing boats. The chemistry in the air was almost electric with excitement as we watched the marchers and floats go by.

John and I Go Outside

Our Aunt Nell had an operation in July and came to stay with her sister, our mum, to recover. Our house on 3rd Avenue was not large enough for all of us so our parents made plans for John and I to fly south and stay with friends outside. The plan was simple; we would fly down at the beginning of August and stay for a few weeks, until our friends parents got tired of us, and then fly home before Labor Day and the start of school. Juneau's new airport terminal was under construction—a two-story building with real waiting lounges. Not nearly as big as Seattle's, but a real improvement over the little one they had when we first arrived. Statehood and progress will do that to you if you're not careful.

"You guys take care of yourselves," mom said, "do as Claire and Gloria tell you, and don't get into any trouble. Your father won't be there to help."

"Don't worry, mom," I said. "I'll take good care of John."

"I don't want to hear anything but good things from Claire and Gloria," dad said, "and stay out of trouble." Sounded like a broken record.

We didn't have the greatest seat on the plane, over the wing so I couldn't look out at the islands and forests as we flew south, but it was also next to the emergency exit so we had extra legroom. The Boeing Strotcruiser's four engines' roared to life and the plane spun around and began taxing out onto the runway. We waved to mom, dad, and Aunt Nell as the plane rolled past onto the runway. You know how it is when the big airplane bounces as it rolls along the ground.

"Whacha doing." John asked as he watched me fiddle with window latch.

"Nothing," I replied, "Just reading these instructions." *Slow rolling bounce.*

"I'm gonna 'tell mom."

"Mom's not here, stupid." I reminded him. *Then a nice rollie bounce.*

"I'm gonna 'tell the stewardesses then."

"Come on, I'm not doing anything, just reading the instructions." *A series of long slow rollie bounce.* "See, 'In case of emergency pull leaver down across window and . . ."

Big bounce!

One thing I should stress with all possible urgency is if you are sitting by an airplane window and the emergency exit is next to you, do not – I repeat – DO NOT - pull the lever that opens the window, especially if the airplane is already taxiing down the runway. Lights flash, horns blare, sirens scream, and the plane comes to a skidding stop!!

The plane returned to the terminal where everybody got off, looking at me like I was some kind of idiot. "What in hell were you thinking?" dad yelled at me (he seldom swore and almost never yelled at us). The PanAm station chief came over and called my dad and mom aside. I don't know what they spoke about, but if you are lucky the pilot may let you back onboard and just move you away from the windows and make you sit in an aisle seat for the rest of the flight. I was lucky, the crew didn't throw me out of the plane and I got to fly south. To this day I don't know why PanAm let me back on the airplane. Nor can I figure out why anybody would be so stupid as to pull the emergency window exit lever as an airplane taxied down the runway? I don't know, maybe because I was 13.

John and I had a great time in Seattle -- the big city—back in America, so to speak. The temperatures were in the high 70°s and mid 80°s, something we weren't used to. When we went swimming in Lake Washington, it was easy to spot John and me in the crowd—our skin was the color of typing paper, while everybody else had a nice tan. The big summer event in Seattle is Seafair and the hydroplane races on Lake Washington. After about two or three hours in the sun, in and out of the lake, John and I looked like boiled lobsters. Noxzema cream put on our burned backs helped a little but even the best of treatments couldn't ease all that pain.

Several things stood out in my mind about Seattle: first, the air stunk from exhaust fumes, and second, it was so crowded and busy. Everybody seemed to want to be someplace else and were in such a hurry to get there. John and I hadn't been gone that long, two and a half years, but it seem that our Seattle friends were so much more sophisticated than we were.

When it was time to go home, neither of us could wait to get back to Alaska. John, Mr. Goody Two Shoes, got to return with one of his friends and their parents, who drove up the Alcan Highway and then took the ferry down to Juneau from Haines. Me? I had to fly home sitting in an aisle seat all the way. I'm sure if the Pan Am crew could have their way, they would have tied me to the seat for the whole flight.

Glacier Ice

A little history here, up until about 1953 or '54, the Alaska Steamship Company ran tourist ships between Seattle and the ports of Southeast Alaska: Ketchikan, Wrangell, Petersburg, Sitka, Juneau, and Skagway. Skagway had its railroad, the White Pass and Yukon connection to Whitehorse and the Yukon Territory and Klondike Gold Fields. When I say "tourist ships," I mean ships like the old *MS Alaska* or *MS Denali*—vessels that carried maybe two hundred passengers at the most, and when they docked, were the only ship in port. A scene far different than the thousands of tourists who pour off the five or six ships that now dock each day during the tourist season. But the Alaska Steam's ships were built between the wars and had a lot of miles on them. They were small, old fashioned, and lacked the amenities of other passenger ships of era, plus they were all painted black.

By 1959 there were no more tourist ships, although some passengers did ride up on the freighters, such as the *MS Susitna*, and most of the passengers were businessmen or government employees, not really tourist.

The tradition of Juneau kids selling ice from Mendenhall Glacier to tourists off the ships that came north during the summer season went back many years. Well, my friends and I were still willing to show Alaska Steam's passengers a bit of our unique lifestyle. One of the things we did to make their visit more authentic and memorable was to greet them as they got off the boat and try to sell them glacier ice. "It's a special kind of ice," we'd say in our pitches. "Blue ice from the Ice Age," we would continue, "I promise this ice will keep your drinks cold forever."

I know we could never get away with anything like that today—not only would the city want to tax us, but the FDA would probably want to inspect our ice for contaminants, and the EPA would probably make us fill out tons of paperwork to verify we weren't depleting the glacier of ice. Life was so much easier back then.

"You know," we told the passengers, "the ice is blue because over the millions years since it formed, about half of the oxygen got squeezed out of the snow crystals." We would pass chunks of crystallized glacial ice around to those who were curious or just good sports. "Water is simply H_2O," we'd say, "but glacier ice has less oxygen than water and, therefore, is not technically ice."

I mean, it sounded good to me, and we sold a lot of ice at 10¢ to 15¢ for a chunk. We told them they could keep it in the ship's freezers until they got back to the States. Never got any complaints, so I guess our customers did okay. We charged an extra nickel if there were ice worms in the chunks (see the part about the FDA above).

To get the ice a couple of guys would ride out to the glacier then hike out onto the ice to fill cardboard lined boxes with "blue ice" (cardboard is a good insulator). Getting blue ice wasn't easy as one would think, and more than one person broke bones in slips and falls on the ice over the years. First off, it had to be clean ice, which meant it couldn't be on the surface—we had to dig for it. Secondly, it had to be old ice, which meant it had to be deep within the glacier. Back then, the face of Mendenhall Glacier came out to about today's tourist parking lot, so it was easy enough for us to hike up the glacier to where the crevasses were. Like the gold prospectors of old, we gathered our pick hammers and cardboard buckets and went prospecting, though this time, we were in search of ice instead of gold. I think OSHA would have a fit today.

On sunny summer days, families would head out to Mendenhall Valley to swim in Dredge Lake (Gastineau Channel was way too cold), maybe do a little fishing in Auke Lake or one of the streams, regardless, such days generally involved a picnic, which was always a good thing.

One particular Saturday, a bunch of us hiked about a half mile up the glacier looking for the good stuff, because this was the last weekend before school started and our last chance to meet the passengers off of the boat. We made our way up the south side of the glacier and then worked our way along the upper edge of the ice, looking for crevasses with deep blue ice in them. When we found what we thought would be a safe crevasse some of the braver guys crawled in and started chipping away. On this particular day I lost my sunglasses down a crevasse, and although it was overcast (it always seemed to be overcast over the glacier), the light rays reflected off a million ice crystals, which acted like little prisms, amplifying the power of the sun's rays. A mile or so on a glacier is a long way with no sunglasses, and by the time we got back to the parking lot, my eyes hurt so much the guys tied a hanky over my eyes and poured cold water over them.

Snow blindness—that was the diagnosis, and for the next two weeks it kept me blindfolded and confined to the house while my mom medicated my eyes. I ended up staying home for the first two weeks of school, which I would never have admitted to missing until I had to miss them (does that make sense?). Snow blindness can be permanent, but I was lucky; the symptoms lasted for about a year. I never had the chance to hike on Mendenhall Glacier again.

The Eight Grade

Of course it was all too soon that we were recalled from our summer craziness and forced back to school. Eight-grade was just as memorable as the seventh, which is to say not much happened. I was well on my way to become a C+ student, which didn't make my folks happy since John was mostly an A student.

Soon after school started John and I were called to the principal's office. It wasn't the first time for either of us, but for once neither knew why we had been summoned. As far as we knew, we were innocent. We were told we could leave school and go across the street to meet our dad in the State Building, the old Federal Building, where he worked. We had no idea what, if anything, we had done. When we got there, dad met us in the big lobby wearing a civilian suit and said we would be going upstairs for a ceremony. Whoa? In three years of visiting the State Building to get our mail at dad's office I had never ventured beyond the ground floor. The courts and the Territorial Legislator had their offices upstairs. We ended up on the fifth floor, in the Superior Court Courtroom. Finally dad told us what was going happening, our mom had passed her U.S. citizenship exams and was going to be sworn in as a new American citizen.

Somehow, it had never occurred to me that my mother wasn't a U.S. citizen. I knew she was British, being born in England and all, but I too was born in England, and I had been an American citizen all my life. The funny part was I didn't even know she had been studying for her citizenship exam; all this time I thought she was trying to help me with history homework. Good going Mom! Following the ceremonies in that beautiful Superior Court room, the VFW hosted a reception for all the new citizens and the first thing my mother did after becoming a U.S. citizen was to join the VFW Auxiliary. John and I weren't in trouble after all.

One of the great things about the Territory of Alaska was at the age of 14 you could get a special "learners" driving permit. My dad had already taught me how to drive a car, but this permit allowed small horsepower motorbikes like Mopeds and scooters like Vespas and Cushmans, to be driven by fourteen-year-olds. "But mom, all the kids are getting one" was the common plea. I figured it would be easier than asking to become a blood brother to a Tlingit, but I had already pulled off that one.

We would say things like "I'll pay for it myself and be real careful." The same discussion went on in most of the homes with fourteen-year-old boys. Eventually somebody's parents gave in, and our comments became more like "Dick's dad got him a moped for his birthday" or "Dwayne's got a new motorbike." My mom and dad were real hard sells, and money was still tight, but I finally convinced them their eldest son needed some form of motorized transportation so he could expand the area where he babysat for family, friends, and neighbors. My argument worked!

Some of us remember taking our Savings Bond stamp books to school on Mondays and buying stamps for 10¢ each, and when we had $18.50 worth of stamps, we would turn in the full books for a $25.00 Savings Bond (of course you couldn't get the $25.00 for ten years, but we didn't quite understand that part). It was time to get serious about saving, so my dad and I went down to B. M. Behrends Bank and set up a savings account in my name. I got a savings passbook in which the teller wrote each of my deposit and the interest earned. This responsibility had all the trappings of adulthood, and I thought it was a pretty big deal.

By the time my birthday rolled around in November, a number of my friends had already gotten motorbikes. For my fourteen birthday, I got to pick out a motor scooter from the Sears and Roebuck catalog. It would be for both Christmas and my birthday. I selected a blue-and-white Cushman motor scooter, which we had shipped to us. November in Juneau is not the ideal time to learn to ride, because of the ice, rain, snow, and curvy, narrow streets. There were restrictions, too. I could have no passengers except for my brother John, who held on for dear life. Nobody wore helmets; there weren't any for bikers back then. My motor scooter was so noisy and clanged so much that my friend Suzie named it Sylvester after the cat of "I thot I taw a paddy tat" fame. I even had decals of Sylvester on the sides. Riding out the Glacier Highway and around Mendenhall Loop Road, I felt the way Mr. Toad must have felt in his automobiles—free.

1960

Although Douglas was off limits because I wasn't allowed to ride my scooter across the bridge because of the ice and snow and because the grade was so steep, new places of discovery opened up. On nice days I would ride out as far as Auke Bay and Mendenhall Valley with its swimming hole at Dredge Lake, all north of town. Closer to home, I enjoyed riding to the fishing-boat marina and the Coast Guard sub port (I never understood why they called it the sub port, as the Coast Guard didn't have submarines and I never saw one tied up there).

I liked the Alaska Steamship Dock when a ship was in port. It was at the end of South Franklin Street near were mom worked so I could go down and enjoyed the way the longshoremen used the deck cranes and derricks to load and unload the cargo; there were no shipping containers. Almost everything in Juneau had to be shipped up by the Alaska Steamship Company. Watching the ships being loaded and unloaded kind of reminded me of the banana boats in the filmstrips we watched back in the 5th grade in geography classes (of course, our longshoremen weren't singing any "Banana Boat Song").

My First Funeral

I went to my first funeral that spring. It was for the daughter of one of my father's coworkers. Her name was Jennie; and she was the middle of five girls and in the fourth grade. We were close to the family and I babysat her and her sisters often. They lived in a big house on the dock next to the Douglas Bridge, where the new bridge now sits. Her family often shared holidays with us and other ACS families. One of her sisters, I can't remember which one, broke her leg and was laid up for a long time. To keep her happy I bought her a parakeet, or budgie as my mother called them, that's how close our families were The saddest part about Jennie's death was the fear that haunts all military families: knowing that in a year or two another set of orders would come and the family would move away, leaving their baby all alone in the cemetery with nobody to care for her grave. It was a sad time for all of us and all the military families in Juneau. I never really thought to ask what Jennie died of, one day she was fine, the next she was in hospital, about a week later she died. It wasn't until many years later that my folks told me Jennie had a reaction to the bites of mites that lived on parakeets, *psittacosis*, or something. For a long time after that I carried that guilt around with me. Most of that has passed now.

For me mum's 30th birthday dad, John, and I decided to get her a nice birthday cake. I'm sure we bought it because I can't imagine any of us guys baking one, besides our kitchen was too small. I do remember getting her a nice present and putting the candles on the cake. Thirty is a big deal you know and John and I put the candles on, and gave Richard the last one to go on. The cake was so pretty on the kitchen table with all 31 candles aglow. Oops, 31 candles! To make up for out little error we put 31 candles on her next birthday cake and the next and the next. I never knew my mother's age; to me she was always 31.

I had my first real date with Susan, Jack's sister, a double date of course, actually four or five nervous, giggly teenage couples, That first movie was Pat Boone's *April Love* and afterwards we all went to Percy's Drug Store soda fountain for shakes and fries. If this sounds kind of '50s-ish, well it was. There were other movie dates as my nerves and poise improved. I remember going to see *Thunder Road* and Elvis Presley's *Love Me Tender*. Most of the girls cried when Elvis got shot, but the guys cheered.

One of my favorite TV shows, *Our Miss Brooks*, was about a high school teacher and the problems she had with her boyfriend – another teacher, the school administrators, and her students. That was my simple impression of high school; it was pretty much my impression of junior high—sort of laid back, with happy teachers and happy students. But in reality, even at jolly ole Juneau Junior High things were not all that rosy.

One incident sticks clearly in my mind because I was there when it occurred, and it became the only time that I knew a student who got expelled from school. It happened during our final classroom period near the end of the school year, on one of those rare spring days when we had the windows open to catch the warm breeze. Our teacher was at the blackboard, going through some problems, when one of the boys started harassing one of the girls at the back of the room. The teacher, of course, asked him to stop, but the student just looked at our teacher and told him where he could go. Even though most of us didn't use that kind of language, we all knew what he meant. Things progressed downhill quickly from there, and the teacher ordered the rest of the students to leave the classroom. Most made a mad dash for the doors to get out, while others lingered a little to see what would happen, but we too got booted, and the doors closed. From the hall we could hear the sound of chairs and desks being thrown about and then the sound of one of the windows being broken. We were afraid one or the other had gone out the window, because we were on the second floor. Quickly, other teachers and staff arrived and put an end to the fight.

When we returned to the classroom the place was in shambles. Desks and chairs were overturned, maps had been torn from the walls, and books and papers were scattered all over the place. After helping the staff pick up the room, we went back to our desks and just kinda sat there in stunned silence for a minute or two, and then it seemed we all wanted to talk at the same time. Both our teacher and the student were gone. What had just happened? I mean why? I think what shook me up the most, more than the fight itself, was thinking about who would dare to take on one of our male teachers? These were guys we really looked up to, these were—the guys who'd won WWII—and they were our heroes.

The student was older than the rest of us in the eighth grade, as he'd flunked a grade or two, and because he was older and bigger than the rest of us we tended to avoid him if we could. You know, he just didn't fit in with any of our groups. I think now that may have added to his problems.

A teacher - student classroom brawl did not happen every day, not at the high school and surely not at our junior high. Sure, we thought of ourselves as tough and maybe a little uncouth, and we had swagger 'cause we were Alaskans. We grew up seeing Indians, loggers, fishermen, and miners come into town and blow their whole paycheck in a single weekend, and we watched as their buddies got them back to the boat, plane, or whatever.

When I told my dad about the fight he reminded me of my own and asked me not to judge the student. The kid probably look around and saw that he needed to do something, strike out at someone, to get help and try to change his fate. He did, but in the end he ended up being sent to reform school outside of Anchorage.

The school year was rapidly coming to a close, and we were looking forward to going on to high school next year. Most of my friends would become Juneau High School Crimson Bears; I, on the other hand, because my dad got orders again, would be going to a new school in Seattle with no friends and no one to rely on. Getting transferred out of Alaska was not as thrilling as getting transferred in.

At the end of the school year we had the eighth-grade Class of 1960 Prom. "White sport coats and pink carnations," and all that stuff. We had had several sock hops at the Teen Club during the year and my mom always made me go, although I didn't always dance. But a Prom is different; for one thing we had to wear shoes. It was held in the junior high gym, which the girls and a few guys had fixed up. Even though we'd learned ballroom dancing in school, none of guys were really all that anxious to be the first one on the dance floor. After two or three dances with only girls on the dance floor, the DJ had a ladies' choice, and was I surprised when Michelle came over and asked.

"Mr. Wright, would you care for this dance?" she asked in a formal manner.

I have never been able to figure out our relationship (if one even existed). I hadn't seen her much except in class, and we never went on a date. She asked me if I still had the bow tie she had knitted for me and of course I said "yes." The highlight of the prom was dancing with Michelle, and after so many years, finally getting to kiss her.

One Last Summer

Alaska wasn't the last state admitted to the Union after all, as Hawaii came in August 21, 1959. We couldn't let that spoil our pride in Alaska's statehood though, and a number of companies and groups around Juneau had statehood parties with Hawaiian themes—you know, with paper palm trees, coconuts, grass skirt and Hawaiian shirt costumes, that sort of thing. I've often wondered how many groups in the lower 48 had Alaskan-statehood-themed parties after we became a state - you know with paper igloos, totem poles, kuspucks, moose, and polar bears.

One of my friends was able to get a hold of the decorations and costumes that Pan Am used for their Hawaiian party and decided to put them to good use—once again at the expense of the Alaska Steamship Company's passengers. Hawaii's star was added that summer of 1960, so five or six of us showed up on the steamship's dock dressed in Hawaiian shirts and shorts the girls had hula skirts which were all too big for them and we tacked up fake palm trees on the buildings and played ukuleles (the Hawaiian music from a portable record player) adding a little extra zing for our friends selling ice. We knew deep down that these passengers really had wanted to go to Hawaii but had been forced to come to Alaska by their evil employers, so we tried to put a little fun in it—and get extra tips, of course.

That last summer in Juneau I got to go on a weekend fishing trip with my dad, some of his army buddies, and two other teenagers, high-school kids whom I didn't know well. We took four boats south to Taku Inlet and then up the fjord for twenty or thirty miles to a stream flowing in from the south and a lake with two Forest Service cabins, East Turner Lake. There was a small dock and float at the landing where we could tie up, but it could only handle two boats at a time. "Here, Bud—you stay with the boats," my dad said, "and make sure they don't get stranded high and dry." As the tide went out and the others carried our gear to the cabin I continued to unload gear from the boats. The tidal range in Taku Inlet is more than twenty feet, and I had to keep moving the boats so they wouldn't get hung up on the rocks.

The winds coming off the glaciers were unbelievably cold even in July, and I had to slosh around in the icy water. Taku Inlet is a magnificent place all wilderness and pristine. I walked up the shoreline a short ways and realized for the first time I was truly out in the Alaskan wilderness alone with only my trusty little .22 rifle. I knew I could drop a deer, but the gun would be no match if a bear came wandering along—and there were bears. Walking back to the boats I heard the croaking of frogs in the bushes along the stream and from the muskeg, and I remembered what Mr. T had told me: "Frogs are magical creatures, you know—just in case you need them."

After a while the others came back and we tied up the two big boats to the float and beached the two smaller ones above high tide, and hiked back to the cabins. But while I sitting there listening to the frogs I started thinking; funny thing about life, I had lost track of Michael and Sonja. After moving across the Channel to Juneau, I had seldom gone back to Douglas. Somebody told me they'd moved back to Angoon to be with their mother. Could be.

We spent two days and nights at the cabins fishing for trout and steelhead. I had better luck with the trout than the steelhead, and my dad's army buddies told a lot of great stories around the woodstove. The army had decided to deactivate the ACS, and these men knew this would be their last outing together. Some of them had served with each other for twenty years or more. The stories were great; including tales about famous people they'd met or helped over the years, such as Lowell

Thomas of *Lawrence of Arabia* fame, who visited Juneau often on his Alaskan trips. It seemed all the guys had stories about him on the North Slope, in the Aleutians, or on Mount McKinley. I even met him twice on his visits to Juneau. There were stories about Bob Hope's tours—not only in Alaska but also during the war in the South Pacific—and stories about hunting and fishing trips that had happened decades ago.

There were stories closer to home too, like the time my dad and Sergeant Deakle (I think they might have been corporals back then) were stationed at Naknak in Bristol Bay and used the station's fishing boat, *Ptarmigan*, to go hunting on another island. They beached the boat, but when they got back it was gone. They were so mad, thinking someone had taken it, until they realized they hadn't beached it high enough and the tide had taken it out. This happened back in 1953, the year Richard was born, and my dad laughed because about three months earlier, the Coast Guard report that *Ptarmigan* had been sighted drifting off the coast of Chile. Other great stories made their way around the woodstove those two nights. Bright and early Sunday morning, after a breakfast of trout and eggs, we were off again to catch the outgoing tide to aid us in our trip back to Juneau. That was the best time I ever had with my dad and I learned so much about a WW II veteran who never really opened up about his military service. About the only thing I knew was that he served in England was assigned to SHAFE, and he married mum.

As expected, my dad got orders, because 1960 marked the end of his four-year overseas tour. Some of the army guys would stay, but most were transferred to other outfits. A lot of my friends' fathers would also get transferred, some stateside. Some, whose fathers worked for the new state would get new positions in Anchorage or Wasilla. Jack and Susan's father also got transferred, but they left after us. Of course most of my friends' families were real Juneauites and didn't move at all.

The last ritual, for us boys moving away, was the "sinking of the fleet". Families were always moving out of Juneau, and some of the teenage boys would take their models; ships, planes, cars, and other models to the tailings below the AJ mine and declare war upon them. When this occurred, maybe a couple times a year, your special friends were invited because this was a private solemn event; the destruction of so many things you loved and took pride in building and painting. We would ride our scooters or motorbikes to the tailings where the ship models would be ballasted so they would float, while the other models would be placed on the far side of one the many depressions on this, the site of Juneau's Million Dollar Golf Course. There were no greens of course because of the chemicals used in the extraction of the gold killed anything that tried to grow. It was a barren wind swept landscape that we chose to destroy our precious models because *HMS Bounty* or *USS Arizona* would not fit into a suitcase, nor would your B-17 bomber, or that totally customized 1962 Ford. Space and weight were at a premium and the army was not going to pay to ship your "toys" back to the states, so we would take our rifles and shoot them, sinking the ships, and blasting the planes and cars to smithereens. It was fun, especially if the models were not yours, but when my time came there was a curtain pain in blasting my favorite ships to the bottom of the sea. It was just another part of army life, you couldn't take with you those things others kids took for granted, having these items around you.

Way too soon dad's orders came, and it was our time to move. But amid all of the packing and confusion of moving, dad took time off to take John and me for one final fishing trip, the Golden North Salmon Derby. The Derby is held over several weekends each June, and for the weekend we went out I won first prize for the largest salmon caught by a teenager. My salmon weighed in at about twenty-four pounds and first prize was $50.00! Unfortunately we left town before the Derby ended so I missed the awards ceremony and my first television appearance. But hey, they put the check in the mail.

The time had come at last. The car and furniture were packed and ready to be shipped, and in true Wright family tradition my brothers and I packed our old army footlockers with all our stuff. Inside my footlocker, wrapped in white tissue paper, lay my most prized possession: a small cedar carving of a frog given to me by Michael, my Tlingit blood brother.

My Frog Totem

Comments and Acknowledgments

This is my story. When I arrived in Juneau, I was a skinny 10-year-old who went by Raney, and when I left four years later, I was older and wiser and known as Bud (one should never have to live through junior high with a name like Raney). The challenges faced by today's youth are different, harder than those we faced in the 1950s, but our experiences growing up are similar; we all have to grow in our own time and space, learn to accept different cultures, different life styles, and figure out how to interact with the opposite sex, and of course, our parents. It's not always easy. This story is about growing up in America but not really in America, at a time and place that existed only once in a lifetime: Alaska on the eve of Statehood.

I was born in England, the son of an American GI and a British war bride. My parents settled with my father's people in North Carolina after the war and my brother John was born in Concord, NC. There was little work with all the GIs returning, so my dad reenlisted in the army and ended up in a little known Signal Corps unit, the Alaska Communications System, ACS—or, as my dad and his buddies, liked to call it, the *McHale's Navy* of the army. Almost at once the army sent us to Seattle, Washington, where my brother Richard was born. For the next fifteen years my dad shuttled between Seattle and various duty stations in the territory. In 1956 my mom, my brothers, and I got to go with him to Juneau.

I went to kindergarten and four different grade schools before our move to Alaska and three high schools after we left. My four years in Juneau were the defining years of my life.

After serving in Vietnam with the navy and using the GI Bill at Central Washington State College, I moved back to Alaska, married, picking up an instant family, and spent fifteen years as a real-estate appraiser out of Ketchikan. Between real-estate appraising and my activities with the Veterans of Foreign Wars and American Legion, I visited a number of native villages and made friends with many Tlingit, Haida, and Tsimshian natives. Our two daughters and three granddaughters still live in Alaska and this book is for them. Like so many "grandpa books" before it, it started out as a story for the grandkids then took on a life of its own.

How does one acknowledge the help you get when you don't know the names of the people who helped you? Most of the people who knew these stories of my family are gone, but there are several sources I would like to acknowledge:

- the staff of the Juneau-Douglas Museum and the Alaska State Archives
- *Growing Up In Juneau*, which helped jog my memory and verify some of it
- *Touring Juneau* by Toni Croft and Phyllice Bradner
- *Tlingit Myths and Texts* by John R. Swanton

- the folks I talked to in the bars and restaurants and at all Alaskan picnics I went to who told me stories about the last frontier
- the Internet and Wikipedia

Which brings us to the names in the story—all of the people I mentioned in the book are real people, and most of the names are correct, but who knows about the spelling? There are no bad guys in my book—okay, maybe one—because I was a kid and really didn't hang around bad guys.

Finally, how does one read most of their way through *The World Book Encyclopedia*? It's like web surfing—at the end of each entry is a list of other topics. One has only to keep moving from one topic to another—reading each, and looking at the additional topics at the end, and choosing another one to keep going. Of course I didn't read the long articles, like entries for each state or country, but there are hundreds of short items that can fill one's brain.

I wish I had more photographs to include, and don't ask me why most of the pictures are winter scenes.

A Frog's Tale is the story of growing up in Douglas and Juneau, Alaska during the quite days prior to statehood

Being an army brat wasn't all that easy. Some duty stations were better that others, then in 1956, when I was ten, my father got transferred again. This wasn't anything new, but still the idea upset me a little. I mean geez, here I am at the top of my form on a Little League team, in Cub Scouts, and I had a bunch of friends and everything. Then my dad told us where we were going, Alaska! Wow that changed everything, for me at least. This would be a real move, Alaska!

The Author at Mendenhall Glacier

Imagine growing up in a small town in Alaska during the middle of that last century, that town being the territorial capitol with statehood just around the corner and all the excitement that that transition would bring? A Frog's Tale is such a story, with humor, sadness, and family love.

Returning to Alaska after serving in Vietnam and graduating from Central Washington State College, Raney traveled widely within the state and extensively throughout Southeast Alaska visiting towns, and villages, getting to know the Natives, their history, and legends.

Printed in the United States
By Bookmasters